3/97

CULTURES OF AMERICA

# RUSSIAN AMERICANS

By Steven Ferry

BENCHMARK BOOKS

MARSHALL CAVENDISH

**Benchmark Books**
Marshall Cavendish Corporation
99 White Plains Road
Tarrytown, New York 10591-9001, U.S.A.

© Marshall Cavendish Corporation, 1996

Edited, designed, and produced by Water Buffalo Books, Milwaukee

The producers gratefully acknowledge the following people for their help in the creation of this book: Bishop Hilarion, Peter
Budzilovich, Dr. Ludmilla Jasenovic, Dr. Anatol Glenn, Boris and Ludmila Maximov, Prof. William Parson, Prof. Anatole
Sokolosky, Mr. and Mrs. Ralph Krupskia, Donna Williams, and Linda Ginn.

**Picture Credits:** Sabine Beaupré 1995: 7, 19; © The Bettmann Archive: 8, 9, 10, 11, 12, 13, 15, 52, 71 (both), 72, 75;
© 1995, Danny Daniels/Alaska Stock Images: 48; © Hazel Hankin: 37; © Richard B. Levine: 40, 42; © Paul M. Perez:
43, 44; © Reuters/Bettmann: 6, 17, 74; © Frances M. Roberts: 1, 34, 61, 62; © H. Armstrong Roberts: 14; © Marina
Samovsky: Cover, 4, 35, 36, 38, 46; Courtesy of Anna and Russel Shtivelberg: 58; © Katrina Thomas: 39, 51, 53, 54, 55,
56, 60, 64, 65; © UPI/Bettmann: 18, 20, 22, 23, 24, 25, 27, 30, 31, 32, 49, 50, 66, 67, 68, 69, 70, 73

**Library of Congress Cataloging-in-Publication Data**

Ferry, Steven
    Russian Americans / by Steven Ferry.
      p.  cm. -- (Cultures of America)
    Includes bibliographical references and index.
    Summary: Provides a history of Russian immigration to the United States and discusses Russian customs and contribu-
tions to American culture.
    ISBN 0-7614-0164-4 (lib. bdg.)
    1. Russian Americans--Juvenile literature. [1. Russian Americans.] I. Title. II. Series.
    E184.R9F47         1995                      95-11026
    973'.049171--dc20                           CIP
                                            AC

To PS – MS

Printed in Malaysia
Bound in the U.S.A.

# CONTENTS

# INTRODUCTION

To most Americans, Russian culture may seem slightly mysterious or unknown. This is the result of three factors that have prevented Russian immigrants from presenting a clear image of their culture.

First, people of over one hundred different nationalities and a variety of different religious and political groups live in Russia. The Russians who came to America over the last two centuries have been members of these different groups, which were often at odds with each other. To varying degrees, they have clung to their different customs and beliefs. Even the Russian Orthodox Church in this country has split into two branches. One uses Russian in an effort to maintain the Russian culture, and the other uses English because it wants to communicate its beliefs to the more Americanized Russian immigrants.

Second, the early Russians in America came to start a new life and wanted to become Americans. Instead of organizing to preserve their culture, several generations of Russian Americans have tried to blend in, many to avoid being thought of as Soviet Communists.

Third, the government in the former Soviet Union, of which Russia formed the largest part, did not allow ethnic Russians to leave their country for seventy years, from the early 1900s until the late 1980s. As a result, Russians have no strong, commonly held identity in America. Instead, many groups of Russian Americans around the country work to keep their specific cultures alive. These groups, while they have their geographical and historical roots in Russia, are made up of people who come from a variety of ethnic, religious, and even racial backgrounds. Perhaps the only thing that loosely binds them together is their common language and motherland. One of these groups, for example, Russian Jews, makes up close to half the current population of Americans with Russian roots. But their culture is primarily Jewish rather than Russian, and perhaps the only thing that binds them and other minorities from the former Soviet Union together is their common language and motherland.

Today, the many different groups of people from Russia enjoy the freedom to practice their own beliefs and live their own lives in America. After years of the Cold War, during which the governments of the United States and the Soviet Union were at odds, it is fascinating and rewarding to see how much the culture of the Russian people has made its mark on life in America today.

These demonstrators are holding their rally outside the Kremlin, a structure that dates back to the twelfth century. It is still in use today as the building that houses Russian government offices.

x

x

# LEAVING A HOMELAND
## A MAGNIFICENT BUT CRUEL COUNTRY

**R**ussia is the biggest country in the world. It is twice the size of Canada, with eleven time zones, compared to North America's five. Russia is also a very beautiful country, with all the physical features any land has to offer: vast plains, towering mountains, desert, seas, lakes, and tundra.

This huge land has a wealth of natural resources, too, but many of them are hard to reach because of harsh weather conditions and the lack of roads. The winters are bitterly cold: In Siberia, to the east, the average January temperature is -50°F. In fact, more than half of Russia is covered with snow for half the year. Although it has a lot to give its people, the land has always been a harsh one to live in.

### Centuries of Suppression

But the climate is not the worst problem most Russians have had to deal with through the ages. In 1547, Ivan the Terrible decreed that he, the czar, was the absolute ruler of all Russians and formed his own secret police to enforce his laws. From then on, anyone who disagreed with the czar's policies or who was suspected of crimes of disloyalty was punished or imprisoned by the secret police. Even minor violations of the law could result in exile to the frozen wastelands of Siberia.

**From before the Russian Revolution in 1917 to the breakup of the Soviet Union a few years ago, emigration from this vast land has occurred in several "waves" over the last century.**

## WHO ARE THE RUSSIANS?

Ethnic Russians are descendants of a Slavic people from Eastern Europe who started the Russian Empire in the city of Kiev, more than one thousand years ago. Today, ethnic Russians make up the majority (85 percent) of the population of Russia. The remaining 15 percent come from over one hundred ethnic minorities, such as the Tartars and Ukrainians, whose countries were conquered by the Russians through the centuries.

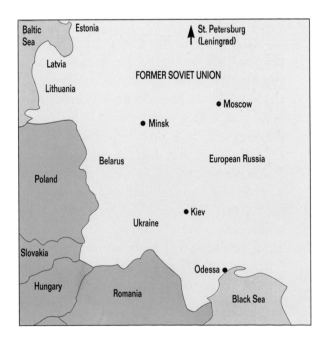

7

Ivan the Terrible was crowned czar in 1547 at the age of seventeen and ruled Russia until he died in 1584. He killed one of his sons with his own hands in 1580.

Ivan the Terrible also ordered that the peasants become serfs, which meant most Russians lost their freedom. Like slaves, serfs farmed the land for nobility or landowners. But because they were allowed to own some property and do as they wished in their own time, they were not absolute slaves.

With these two decrees, the Russian people were controlled and deprived of their rights for nearly 450 years. The czars who came after Ivan, right up until the 1917 revolution (which combined Russia with several other republics to form the Soviet Union), prevented their country from developing with the rest of Europe and the Americas. As a result, Russian industry, political systems, medicine, technology, and living conditions were primitive when Russians started to emigrate to the United States in the second half of the nineteenth century.

## Huts for Houses and Not Much to Eat

For the peasants who lived and worked in the country, life in Russia remained almost as basic at the end of the nineteenth century as it had been hundreds of years before. Whole families lived in one-room, wooden huts with thatched roofs and giant clay ovens, six feet high by twelve feet wide, that dominated the room. In the summer, the children would sleep outside the hut. But during winter nights, the family would bring the pigs, cows, and horses into the hut, close the windows, and actually climb into the oven, which had ledges built into it for beds. The heat still in the oven from the day's cooking kept them warm while they slept.

The peasants usually ate rye bread, potatoes, dairy products, and the few vegetables grown during the short summer season. The crops often failed, however, and thousands of people would starve, as happened in 1891 and 1909. Most families were too poor to afford meat, and those who had animals either worked them in the fields or raised them to sell.

The men labored all day in the fields, using horses harnessed with rope to wooden plows. The women milked the cows, fed the animals, cooked, cleaned, cared for the children, and worked in the fields during the summer.

Russian peasants labor in the fields at the turn of the century. Men, women, and children alike all had specific jobs to do, and children often missed months of school in order to help their parents.

The children helped in the fields by the time they were eleven or twelve. The few who attended school studied only during the four or five months of winter. As late as 1912, with a population of 180 million, only 7 million Russian children were attending school. Even for them, the quality of education was poor, as half of them were unable to sign their names and only a quarter could read. Because it was hard to keep surfaces clean at home with animals in the house, disease was a common enemy that claimed many lives. With one doctor for every twenty-one thousand people in the country in 1912 (in the United States during the same year, there was one doctor for every eight hundred people), the peasants had no medical help available to fight the diseases.

## Repressive Authorities

Life did not have to be so hard, as Russia was immensely wealthy in natural resources and could have supported all its people. But life was made hard for the majority by the minority. Until 1861, 85 percent of Russians were serfs. The landowners actually owned their serfs and listed them as part of their property and

## BUILDING THEIR OWN HOMES

"The house I lived in was made from logs we cut in the forest, with the cracks filled in with mud and clay. The floor was made of mud and each Saturday we put new clay over it to make it look clean. Sometimes we had windows, sometimes we didn't. When we did have a window, it was made of paper."

— Memories of a ten-year-old Russian girl living in the country at the end of the nineteenth century.

Czar Nicholas II is photographed with all five of his children, from left to right: Maria, Olga, Tatiana, Alexis, the czar, and Anastasia. They were executed in 1918 by Russian revolutionaries.

Annual taxes were heavy, sometimes more than a family's total yearly income. This meant the peasants were tied to the land, as they couldn't leave the village until the taxes were paid. The local police could fine and imprison anyone they chose and could enter any house at any time without a warrant. If a building did not meet regulations, they could tear it down. In addition to all these demands and burdens, Russian men had to serve at least five years in the czar's army, often laying down their lives in some far-off land in a war that meant nothing to them.

## The Loss of Land and the Move to the Cities

Although the serfs were given their freedom in 1861 by the reform-minded Czar Nicholas II, they were not given enough land to support their families. In fact, a system of land rotation was enforced by village councils, which meant the farmers did not own the land they worked on: They were allowed to farm land, often only a narrow strip a few yards wide, for only a short while before it was given to someone else. In the last half of the century, the little land they were allowed to harvest was reduced by half, making it impossible to feed their families and forcing some to emigrate or move to the cities and work in factories.

As one Russian said, "The peasants loved the land and the work in the fields, and they loved no other kind of work." So moving to the factories in the cities was not popular. But by 1908, half a million people in Russia

wealth. In most, though not all, cases, they treated the serfs very badly.

Villagers could elect their own local councils, but the landowners and nobility had the power to remove them and subject them, or any other villagers, to various kinds of punishment, such as flogging. If a landowner told a peasant he needed some work done, the peasant would usually not dare ask for payment. And if the peasants needed something from the nobility, such as permission to build a house, they would often have to bribe the nobles to get it.

These impoverished workers, some of them barefoot, pose in front of a dilapidated shed around the turn of the century.

worked in factories, where the conditions were no easier than in the country. They often worked twelve hours a day for seven days a week, at an average pay of twenty rubles a month. With that kind of money, two families might be able to rent one room between them and pay for some food.

## No Real Helping Hand from the Church

Perhaps during this time, the Russian peasants could have found some comfort in their churches. For uneducated farmers used to small and smelly houses, the churches must have been impressive places to visit. They were beautifully decorated and lit by many candles; the sweet smell of incense and magnificent music filled the huge spaces, and the priest, dressed in flowing robes, led them through complex rituals. But although the farmers may have found a hope of spiritual salvation in the churches, they received no real help in improving their conditions on earth.

The Russian Orthodox Church at the time did not provide any community outreach programs to help those in need. Some priests did not even preach; instead, they reported on their parishioners as secret agents for the czar, who actually controlled the Church.

And for those peasants who were not Russian Orthodox but followed some other faith, there was the ever present threat of being driven from their homes or being sent to Siberia.

## How the Peasants Enjoyed Themselves

The Russian peasants did not let this harsh life demoralize them completely though. They sang often, even while they worked. Some evenings, they would get together to sing and play their accordions and balalaikas (a stringed instrument that looked like a triangular guitar). On Sundays and holidays, young men and women would go for walks, playing their music, singing, talking, and dancing as they went. They

Family and friends enjoy some tea and vodka in the 1920s. Note the balalaika (which seems to have only two strings instead of the usual three) and the large samovar, meaning literally "self-boiler," which is used to heat water for tea.

had hundreds of folk songs to choose from about love, war, death, and their beloved countryside.

There were many gala holidays celebrating religious, seasonal, and family events during which they sang and danced. The women dressed in brilliantly colored and embroidered costumes decorated with beads, and the men wore their traditional baggy trousers, long boots, and shirts tied at the waist.

The Russian peasants at that time formed close communities, drawn together by the harsh climate and conditions. They were not rich, but they were sociable and willing to share the little they had, even with a stranger. As one emigrant said many years later in the United States, "Sure, life was tough in Russia, but it is still our native homeland. We didn't have much to eat, and we didn't have any money, but we had friends and family and music, and we were in that sense very rich."

## Different Groups of Emigrés and Why They Left

Because Russian emigration was actively discouraged or absolutely forbidden for centuries, the history of Russians emigrating to the United States has been one of people escaping every now and then, rather than being allowed to leave. But leave they did, mostly in the fifty years between 1870 and 1920, when emigration was permitted technically but made very difficult in practice.

The first Russians to leave for the United States were a few members of the middle classes who wanted to escape the excessive control of their lives by the Russian government during the eighteenth and early nineteenth centuries. This lack of freedom was obvious and painful to many educated Russians. In addition to the actions of the secret police in controlling what people did and their contacts with others, the press was censored. Independent newspapers would publish front pages with just a few sentences on them, the rest having been blocked out by the government. The freedoms we are used to in the United States did not exist for these Russians, and so they left.

## The Oppressed Farmers

Although peasants may have wanted to emigrate, until they were freed from serfdom in 1861 they were not allowed to travel outside the village, let alone leave the country. So there was no large flow of Russian peasants emigrating until the late nineteenth century, when the exodus to the United States eventually started.

In the few decades before World War I began in 1914, nine of every ten Russians who emigrated were peasants. They left

This woman is about to begin her workday beneath the surface of the earth. Both men and women worked as coal miners and were paid the same wage under the new Soviet government following the revolution in 1917.

## RUSSIAN INGENUITY

When emigration was finally allowed by law after 1861, the government made it very hard for poor, illiterate peasants to leave the country. They had to fill out application forms and pay a fee, as well as buy a passport. After so many years of oppressive government, Russians were used to finding ways around rules that were not designed to help them, as illustrated in this story told by a man who eventually made it to the United States: "I was a military agent and couldn't get out of the country. We had very little money, so I couldn't bribe my way out. One of my relations in the United States, who was twenty-six, had an adequate passport. He sent it back in a loaf of bread and I used it to get out. I was almost caught because I was only eighteen, but the guard was drunk and I was drunk. I then sent the passport back to someone else, who followed the same pattern, and so forth. As far as I know, that passport was used at least seven times by different people."

**Two elderly Jewish men study the books of their faith — a practice Russian Jews have clung to despite centuries of persecution.**

because they wanted a better life where they could make a living and be free of the selfish landowners. Most of them did not plan to return to Russia, though some families pooled their resources and sent one male member to the United States so he could come back with money for land, food, tools, and dowries (gifts needed by a bride for the man she marries).

Not many women left Russia at first. When they did, it was sometimes to escape an old tradition whereby parents arranged marriages for their children. A Russian immigrant in the United States recalled many years later: "My mother had been engaged by my grandfather to a man who was thirty years old. My mother was eighteen, and she had never seen her future husband. My mother thought this was a bunch of nonsense and so did her mother, so they stole the money my grandfather had hidden away and my mother was sent to the United States, where she could marry someone she loved."

Religious persecution was another reason that many Russians left their homeland between 1870 and 1914 for the United States. The Mennonites and the Molokans were two Christian religious sects who were driven out, as were Russian Jews, the group most consistently affected by religious intolerance in Russia.

## Russians Jews and the Pogroms

In 1791, the Russian government passed a law restricting Jews to a Western Russian area called the Pale of Settlement. The three million Jews who lived there were restricted to specific towns and were limited by law to certain jobs. They were not allowed to own any land. Despite these restraints, Russian Jews continued their traditional way of life and, because they ran schools for their children, were very literate compared to the Russian peasants.

In 1881, after the reform-minded Czar Alexander II was assassinated, attacks were carried out on these Jewish communities.

Russian peasants, urged by village officials and priests, formed armed gangs and attacked the Jews. Many families were killed, and the rest driven from their homes. These attacks, called pogroms, were repeated in 1903 and 1905, and many Russian Jews sought refuge in the United States.

## Revolution and the Aristocracy

The Russian Revolution began a few years later, in 1917. The revolution was an attempt by Russian leaders like Vladimir Ilyich Lenin, Nadia Krupskaya (Lenin's wife), Aleksandr Kerensky, and Leon Trotsky to improve life for the majority of Russians who had been abused by the nobility for so many centuries.

With the communist revolution, there was a complete change in the type of people who emigrated to the United States. The Russian poor who had formerly sought eco-nomic independence and freedom from sup-pression did not leave, because they thought they would get a better deal from their new government. But the aristocracy and some of the middle class found it necessary to escape when their lives were threatened and their property taken away.

Within the next few years, as the politi-cal changes continued to occur in Russia, moderates and even radicals who had helped bring about the revolution and then dis-agreed with the way communism was devel-oping also fled the country. They were escaping the new secret police, who were executing many Russians and sending others to concentration camps in Siberia.

Most emigrated to Western Europe, especially Paris and Belgrade, but approxi-mately forty thousand went to the United States. Whatever chance the revolution had of succeeding ended when Joseph Stalin

Russian revolutionary leader Vladimir Lenin and his wife, Nadia Krupskaya, enjoy the sunshine in a garden near Moscow in August 1922.

took control. The revolution turned into a nightmare for most of the Russian people. Their country became the largest among many republics forced by the communist government into the new Soviet Union. Many aspects of their culture, traditions, and religion were restricted or forbidden entirely. The government used fear and intimidation to rule its people, and many citizens, wary of the police, became suspicious of their neighbors and turned against one another.

Because Russia was the birthplace of the revolution and most of the people in the Soviet Union were Russians, the rest of the world considered all Russians to be communists and often referred to the Soviet Union as "Russia." But fewer than one in ten Russians were ever members of the Communist Party, and some of these had no choice about joining, as their jobs required membership in the party.

## Stalin and World War II

If the Russians had been suppressed before by the czars, they suffered still more under the dictator Joseph Stalin. He turned the Soviet Union into something approaching a giant prison, from which few managed to escape. Stalin established concentration camps to which thirty million Russian men and women were sent without fair trial and on invented charges. There, they were used as slave labor until they died of starvation, the harsh punishments they received, or the bitterly cold climate.

As a result, between 1930 and 1944, only 14,060 Russians managed to make it to the United States. Those who did told stories of forced labor camps, secret police, starvation, torture, and general oppression.

The next large group of Russians who moved to the United States were the victims of World War II. At the end of the war, eight million refugees from the fighting were stuck abroad and needed to return to their own countries. Of these, thirty-five thousand were Russians who wanted to go to the United States, and their wish was granted when they were sent there between 1947 and the end of 1951. But they were the last to leave Russia freely for the next forty years. During this period, known as the Cold War, the governments of the Soviet Union and the United States, while never actually declaring war, were hostile to each other.

## The Cold War

During the 1960s and 1970s, two groups of Soviet citizens managed to leave their homeland. The first group, Soviet Jews, were allowed to emigrate to Israel, but some, as soon as they were out of the Soviet Union, came to the United States instead. The second category consisted of outstanding artists, performers, scientists, and other celebrities, most of whom defected (left their country and the control of its government without permission). Sometimes the Soviet government would allow professionals to travel to other countries to give performances or go to professional conferences. The government wanted to prove to the world that Soviet artists and scientists were among the world's best. But while on tour outside Russia, some of these professionals escaped from their Soviet chaperones and sought refuge in the embassies of other countries. These dissidents (people who disagree) were unhappy with the restrictions on their lives and careers at home.

One such escapee was Svetlana Alliluyeva, Stalin's own daughter. She wrote several books while in the United States, condemning the harshness of her father's dictatorship.

Customers line up on a Moscow street in January 1992 to buy fruit at record-setting prices after price limits were lifted following seventy years of controls by the former Soviet government.

Other dissidents included the dancers Rudolf Nureyev, Natalia Makarova, and Valery Jalina Banov. They all joined North American and European dance and ballet companies and continued their careers. The poet Joseph Brodsky, the cellist and conductor Mstislav Rostropovich, and scientists Valery Chalidze and Chores Medvedev also made it out.

## The Recent Exodus

Since the collapse of the government of the old Soviet Union in 1991, Russians have been freer to emigrate. Up to a million have come to the United States in the last few years in search of a better life, the majority of them being Russian Jews who have settled in and around New York City.

Although the men and women in Russia and the other republics that used to form the Soviet Union have political and other free-

doms at last, daily life has actually become harder for many of them. They live with such day-to-day problems as the lack of housing in overcrowded cities and the lack of electric power and running water in houses in the countryside. The transportation systems are so inadequate that it is very hard to move merchandise from the factories to the towns, and so there is little for Russians to buy in the shops. Russians sometimes have to stand in long lines to buy food, clothing, or household goods. Increasing crime and corruption also make it hard to prosper in Russia today.

Most of the Russians who left their homeland over the last 130 years have done so to escape political oppression and grinding poverty. They left for America because it promised to solve these problems, but it was not until they arrived that they could discover whether their dreams would come true.

Basilio Tolmasoff was one of six Russian farmers and their families who founded a new Russian community in Ramona, just north of San Diego, California, in 1947. California has historically been a magnet for Russian immigrants to the United States.

# LIFE IN A NEW LAND
## THE PROMISE OF FREEDOM AND PLENTY

For centuries, Europeans had turned to Russia for warm furs to wear in winter. In response, the Russians had to travel farther and farther into the eastern wilderness to find animals with the furs they needed. When they had hunted all the game as far as the Siberian coast, the czar ordered two of his navy ships to continue the search east for new lands and animals.

### The First Russians in America

In 1741, Russian sailors came upon the Aleutian Island chain off the coast of Alaska. There they found more animals than they could have ever imagined. Hunters and traders soon followed, eager to lay their hands on the prized pelts (furs) of sea otters, seals, and foxes. The Russians continued their move eastward until 1763, when they reached Kodiak Island, the easternmost Aleutian Island.

In 1784, the first permanent Russian colony in North America was established by a trader on Kodiak Island. Soon afterward,

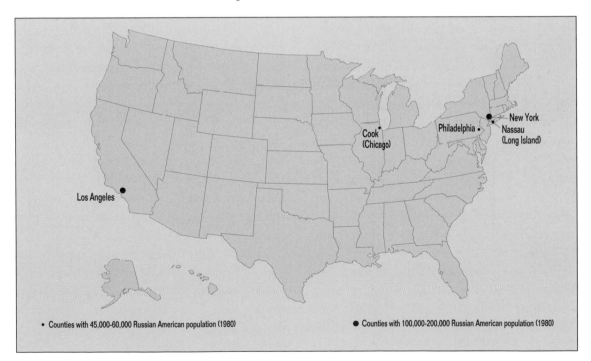

• Counties with 45,000-60,000 Russian American population (1980)     ● Counties with 100,000-200,000 Russian American population (1980)

**Russians first came to North America as colonizers two hundred years ago, settling in Alaska and the Pacific Northwest. Later waves brought Russian immigrants to other part of the United States, particularly California and New York.**

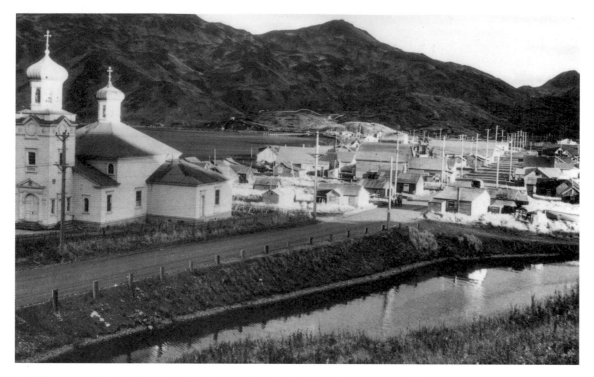

A village near Dutch Harbor, Alaska, on Unalaska Island, one of the Aleutian Islands, in 1943. The spires on the Russian Orthodox church give evidence of this community's Russian heritage.

thirty serfs were sent to settle and farm in Yakutat on the Alaskan mainland. Ten missionaries followed, who built the first Russian Orthodox church in America. The first Governor of Russian Alaska, Alexander Baranov, was appointed in July 1799. He mastered the native Aleuts' language, married an Aleut, and learned to hunt sea otters. Within seven years, nine trading posts and colonies had been established in Alaska and the settlement in Kodiak grew to about forty buildings.

Although Baranov tried to treat the Alaskan Natives fairly, he could be harsh with them on occasion, and he had the poor judgment to establish the capital of Russian America at Sitka, which was in the heart of Tlingit country. The Tlingit were not on especially good terms with the Russians, so when traders from the United States brought rum and firearms to exchange for furs with the Tlingit in 1800, Baranov objected because he knew trouble would follow. The American traders ignored Baranov, and in 1802, the Tlingit attacked and completely destroyed the Sitka settlement, killing or capturing nearly six hundred people. Two years later, Baranov attacked the Tlingit with a Russian warship, drove away the people, and created another settlement, which he called New Archangel.

By the time Russia sold Alaska to the United States in 1867 for 7.2 million dollars, 576 Russian men and 208 Russian women were living in forty-three communities throughout the state. Ironically, Alaska turned out to be worth a lot more than 7 million dollars when oil, tourism, and lumber made the state a gold mine for the U.S. economy.

## RUSSIAN INDUSTRY IN NORTH AMERICA

Russians brought skilled trades to North America very early in their history on this continent. In 1793, they established a brass and iron foundry on the mainland near Sitka, where they made huge bells that they sold to Franciscan missions all the way south in California.

In 1841, to celebrate their discovery of Alaska a hundred years before, the Russians launched the first steam vessel in the Pacific. It was entirely built in the Sitka shipyard, except for a sixty-horse-power engine that came from the United States.

At the time, however, the Russians thought they were getting a good deal because they had already hunted most of the animals. They also thought the British in Canada or even the Americans might try to take over Alaska, and they did not want to get into a fight over the land. Americans, on the other hand, thought the United States was getting a raw deal. Newspapers called the sale "Seward's Folly," after Secretary of State William Seward, who arranged the sale.

For the next seventeen years, Alaska had no real local government, and life there became somewhat lawless and uncertain. Where there were U.S. military units, such as in Sitka, some order was maintained. But when the soldiers left the town in 1877, only twenty families stayed on. The rest left rather than put up with the lack of order. Although Russians living in Alaska were allowed to remain as U.S. citizens if they wanted to, three hundred returned to Russia, some went to Canada, and others preferred the warmer climate of San Francisco. A handful of Russian residents stayed, however, as did thousands of descendants of mar-

## RUSSIANS IN CALIFORNIA

The Russians sent two unsuccessful expeditions from Alaska farther down the West Coast with the idea of setting up more colonies. One expedition to Seattle failed when the ship was wrecked near the Columbia River. The other went to California and might have been successful, had the captain not died on his way back to see the czar in Russia. The captain had won over the heart of the Spanish commander in California by proposing to marry his daughter. The story goes that the daughter waited years for her lover to return before dying of a broken heart.

Despite these setbacks, the Russians did not give up on their idea of setting up colonies in North America. Fort Ross was established eight miles north of the Russian River, near San Francisco, in 1812. Ninety-five Russians and eighty Aleuts arrived there from Sitka to raise agricultural products for the communities in Alaska, where the growing season was very short.

The fort was sold in 1841 for thirty thousand dollars, bringing to an end any official Russian presence in California. All the Russian settlers returned to Sitka.

Three hundred Russian refugees land in Seattle, Washington, in 1923. They are members of a wave of Russians who left their homeland after the revolution.

riages between Russians and Aleuts. Many places in Alaska still have Russian names, such as Baranov Island and the Shelikof Strait.

## Where Russian Immigrants Settled

It is hard to say exactly how many Russian Americans live in the United States today; the number stands at between two and three million. Most of the earliest arrivals were traders and colonists rather than immigrants to an already established nation, and they settled in Alaska and California.

When Russian immigrants did start to arrive during the eighteenth and nineteenth centuries, they went mainly to the northeastern states. Large Russian communities developed in New York City, Philadelphia, Chicago, Buffalo, and Detroit. Smaller Russian communities were established elsewhere in the country during the 1880s and given

Russian names, such as the towns of Odessa in Texas and Washington, and Moscow in Idaho.

A small group of Russian emigrants who had fled to China during the 1917 revolution left for the United States twenty years later when war broke out in the Far East. More followed in 1949, when a communist government took over in China. Both these groups of Russians settled mainly around San Francisco.

Immigrants who followed later also took the same routes, but today, New York is their most common destination. There are also tens and perhaps hundreds of thousands of Russians living in the United States who arrived on student and visitor visas and stayed on as illegal aliens.

## Unskilled Laborers

The first large group of Russian immigrants, mainly peasant farmers looking for a

## PIONEERING RUSSIANS IN THE COLONIES

One of the first known Russians to emigrate to North America was Charles Thiel. He changed his name to Charles Sist and published books (one of which was Tom Paine's *The American Crisis*) in Philadelphia in 1769. He also helped discover that anthracite (coal that gives off little smoke) could be used as a fuel. He formed his own mining company, which failed only because he couldn't sell anthracite to people who were not used to it. A century later, however, Americans began to use anthracite, and many Russian immigrants made a living digging it out of the ground in the eastern states.

Another early Russian immigrant was Fedor Karzhavin, who joined the colonial American forces in 1776 as the "Russian American" who helped provide military supplies in the fight against British rule.

better life and better pay, arrived in the eastern states at the end of the nineteenth century. They were almost penniless and did not speak English. Their first concern was to find a job. More than half of them went to work in the factories and mines of New York and Pennsylvania. Employment in a steel mill or coal mine meant hard work for twelve hours a day. One Russian immigrant worked ninety-one hours one week; the rest of the time he traveled to and from work, ate, and slept. "This is how I slave," he said.

Because many Russians lacked industrial skills, they were given the heaviest physical jobs. In the steel mills, they lifted heavy sacks of coal and hauled them to blazing furnaces. In the mines, the hours were shorter, but the working conditions were worse.

**These women and children docking in San Francisco have left many friends and relatives behind in their haste to leave Russia.**

Even though he has been living in the United States for many years, this Russian settler still wears the traditional farmers' clothes of his homeland.

Russian miners never saw the sun, breathed black coal dust that often resulted in lung disease, and were constantly aware of the danger of cave-ins and poisonous fumes. This environment was far from the fresh air and open farmland of Russia that they were used to and loved.

Having the hardest and most dangerous jobs, Russians in factories and mines were often involved in accidents. They were not familiar with U.S. laws, and the companies they worked for did not tell them they were entitled to receive money when they were injured. Many of these Russians were unhappy, especially as they felt the foremen were rude and unfair, giving them the hardest jobs. Many Russian immigrants did not like the country that they had expected to provide the solution to their problems, so they did not bother to learn its language and customs.

Russians who arrived in the United States to own and run their own farms, such as Mennonites who settled in the Midwest, were generally better off than those who went to the factories and mines. At least they were using their old-time farming skills and worked in the fresh air of the countryside.

## Easy Targets

These early Russian immigrants had no familiarity with the operation of a free society like the United States, where people could work in their own businesses, buy each others' products, and manage their own money. They did not know American customs or speak English and could not understand the laws and their rights. Whether they lived in the cities or the countryside, they were easy targets for dishonest people who would twist the facts to suit their own purposes.

Russians who tried to set up their own farms, for instance, were often cheated by realtors who sold them land that was impossible to cultivate. Quack doctors would take advantage of Russian immigrants' distrust of the medical profession to advertise fake medicines and overcharge them for the potions.

Some grocers would overcharge immigrants for the food they bought. Something as simple as a bank account was completely new to the Russians. Many thought a bank was a place to leave money for safekeeping. They had no idea that they were meant to receive interest as well, so some dishonest bankers just gave them their money back without paying interest.

This was not the only trick some banks played on unsuspecting Russian immigrants. One particular swindle involved encouraging them to turn over their savings to the bank. The banks then faked bankruptcy. Corrupt lawyers would tell Russian immigrants that they could recover only half of their savings, and the banks and lawyers then split the rest. In 1917 alone, there were fourteen of these bank "failures" in Chicago. In 1919, lawsuits totaling two million dollars were brought against banks using this swindle in Baltimore. Other banks lent the immigrants money and charged them much higher interest rates than normal. One bank in San Francisco even went to the trouble of printing fake rubles, which they sold to Russian immigrants to send to their families in Russia.

Russian immigrants could have asked the U.S. government and public agencies for help when they were being cheated. But

Russian Americans shopping in the thriving Russian community of Brighton Beach in Brooklyn, New York. Brighton Beach has become a center of Russian American life and culture.

A RUSSIAN HELPING AMERICANS

In 1792, a Russian nobleman called Prince Gallitzin arrived in America and converted to Catholicism. He gave up all claims to his fortune and spent his life in the Allegheny Mountains of Pennsylvania. His charity, bravery, and tolerance became legendary. The town of Gallitzin is named after him, and his church and house in Loretto, Pennsylvania, still stand today.

they were so used to the Russian government betraying them that they distrusted all governments. They had no idea that the U.S. government would act to help them.

## How Early Immigrants Lived

The majority of Russian Americans rented apartments. Some of them would, in turn, rent rooms in their apartments to other Russian immigrants. One family, for instance, rented a three-room apartment in Pittsburgh in 1920 for twenty dollars a month. The family slept in one of the rooms, which had no windows and was heated with a bad-smelling gas stove. They rented out the second room to five boarders, each of whom paid six dollars a month rent, and the third room was shared by everybody as a combined kitchen, laundry, and living room. The rooms were in poor condition, with rags stuffed into the large cracks showing in the walls.

One Russian American woman ran a boarding house for Russian immigrants. She had four rooms that she rented to twenty men, each of whom paid her three dollars a month. She would wash and mend their clothes and cook their dinners, which in her case meant cabbage soup most of the time.

Russian immigrants brought many of their customs and habits with them to this country. Some of these, such as their bathing system, appealed to Americans seeking new ways to entertain and refresh themselves. Russian baths involved heating stones and placing some in a large tub of water. As this heated up the bath water, the other hot stones were sprinkled with water to produce steam throughout the bathroom. The bathers sat in the steam and beat their bodies with birch brooms, which made the heat seem more intense.

Living conditions in city apartments may have been poor, but they were far better

## FREE TIME IN THE UNITED STATES

One hundred Russian men in Chicago were asked in 1910 how they spent their free time. Many of them went to movies, and quite a few spent their time drinking in bars. The rest occasionally read books, listened to or played music, visited the theater, went for walks, played cards, or went to church. The younger ones went dancing with young women. Those men who worked seven days a week were very bitter about having no time off. One of them said, "When we want a good time, we sleep a couple of hours."

Russian women preferred dances and movies. In order to look pretty for their dance partners, they would dress like American movie stars, sometimes spending their hard-earned savings on silks and furs.

This Russian American woman, photographed in 1947, is baking bread just the way Russian women did for hundreds of years. Her clothing, too, is similar to the style worn at the time in the Soviet Union.

than the circumstances endured by the Russian miners, who lived in shantytowns beside the coal mines. Large families were crowded into two-room shacks built of tin cans, tarpaper, and old boards. There were no toilets in these shacks, so they used the ground outside as a bathroom. One miner summed up the entire experience as "not healthy work, all die young. No one live to sixty here."

If the early immigrants in general were not very happy, it is perhaps understandable if one looks at how their lives changed when they came to the United States. Whatever was wrong with Russia when they left, at least they had a healthy, dry climate. In the United States, the climate was either hot and humid or cold and damp. Most of the immigrants went from open fields in Russia to factories and fumes in America. Instead of living in their own overcrowded houses in the Russian countryside, they lived in over-

crowded tenement blocks in U.S. cities, sharing rooms or apartments with strangers.

Although much of the food was not what early Russian immigrants were used to, they certainly did not starve, and they even managed to prepare some familiar dishes. A typical diet included bread with every meal. The daily menu might also include coffee at five in the morning to get the long day going; a breakfast at nine of Polish sausage, ham, and an apple; coffee and steak for lunch at noon; and for dinner at six, cabbage soup followed by half a pound of meat and potatoes.

One thing that Russian immigrants had hoped to enjoy in the United States, which had been denied them in Russia, was the freedom to work at a job of their choice and be paid for it. But the reality of life in the States was that they were tied to their jobs because they could not afford to leave them.

## ST. PETERSBURG, FLORIDA

A Russian exile of noble birth, Peter Dementiev, became a businessman and railroad builder when he arrived in the United States. In 1888, he built a railroad from central Florida to the site of St. Petersburg on the Gulf Coast and helped found the city there. As the story goes, he tossed a coin with his partner to see who would name the city. Dementiev won and named it after his hometown, the capital of old Russia.

Unless forced by prolonged strikes at their factories or general unemployment in their area, the Russian immigrant family at the turn of the century rarely moved to a new job or house in a different community.

## Russian Mennonites in America

Not all the Russian farmers who came to North America went to the factories in the East. About ten thousand German Russians called Mennonites arrived in the United States in the 1870s and settled on farms in the northern Midwest and Great Plains.

The Mennonites were a religious sect founded in Switzerland in 1525 and named for a Dutch religious leader called Menno Simons. One of their beliefs was that men should not go to war. Many of them lived in Germany in the eighteenth century, a time when Germany was constantly at war. Because they were very good farmers, the Russian empress, Catherine the Great, promised the Mennonites they would not have to fight in any wars if they moved to central Russia and farmed the fertile lands there. The German-speaking Mennonites

did very well for a hundred years, until the Russians tried to make them join the Russian army and stop practicing their customs and religion.

The Mennonites decided to leave Russia and sent research teams to the United States and Canada. The Canadian government promised them free transportation from Russia, free land in Manitoba, and freedom from military service. The U.S. government promised only that there would be no wars for the next fifty years. Many Mennonites therefore left for Canada, but thousands of others emigrated to the United States between 1870 and 1914 because the climate in the United States was better for farming than Canada's.

The Mennonites had a smooth trip over, and when they arrived in the United States, fellow Mennonites gave them temporary homes and rest before they went West. The Mennonites traveled by train to towns in Kansas, Nebraska, the Dakotas, and Minnesota, where they bought the land, equipment, and wagons they needed to establish their own farms. Even though their farms were far apart, Mennonite communities built their own churches and schools and remained in close contact with one another.

When the United States went to war against Germany in 1917, Mennonites affected by anti-German feeling believed that they could no longer practice their customs or speak their language. When the U.S. government began drafting Mennonites into the military, they ran into trouble over their pacifist views. Some Mennonites worked in the military as noncombatants, but others would not. They were called cowards and were jailed. A few of them died from the mistreatment they received in jail. In later years, many of their sons and daughters left the farming communities and lost touch with their culture.

The Hutterites, a group of Russian Mennonites in South Dakota, were also badly treated. Even though they had contributed thirty thousand dollars to war relief work, their South Dakota County Council confiscated many of their cattle and sheep and sold them to raise more money for the war. The council also tried to cancel their religious charter, the official document that allowed them to practice their religion. Consequently, after World War I, the Hutterites immigrated to Canada, which they felt had shown much more tolerance of their religious beliefs.

## The Molokans

Another group, the Molokans, also fled Russia between 1905 and 1907 because of religious persecution. They were Protestants who had broken away from the Russian Orthodox Church in the eighteenth century. They were called "Molokans," which is Russian for "milk drinkers," because they drank milk during the Russian Orthodox Church's Lenten fast, when milk was forbidden. The Molokans were also pacifists and so were harassed during the Russian-Japanese War of 1904. Five thousand of them emigrated to North America, settling mainly in Los Angeles, where they tried to preserve their language, diet, and religion. Some of them set up farming communities in southern California.

Unfortunately, they also experienced difficulties during World War I. And as the young Molokans grew up, they became more and more Americanized and abandoned their culture. The older Molokans tried to reestablish their culture by moving away from Los Angeles to northern and central California, but they were unsuccessful, and no trace remains of the Molokan culture in the United States today.

## The Russian Jews

While the Mennonites were leaving Russia at the end of the nineteenth century, Russian Jews were also being forced to leave. Many went to North America so they could live, work, and practice their religion in

## ONE WAY TO MAKE A LIVING

When Mennonite farmers arrived in the Dakotas, they found the virgin soil was too rough for their plows. In order to pay for better ones, they collected all the buffalo bones they found lying on the plains. (In the 1870s, American buffalo herds were wiped out by order of the U.S. government to make way for farmland and cattle, and thousands of buffalo carcasses remained.) The Mennonites sent the bones east, where they were used to make numerous commercial goods, such as glue, fertilizer, and buttons. They were even used as an ingredient to help refine sugar.

In the thirteen years it took to collect all these bones, it is estimated that forty million dollars were paid to people like the Mennonites who gathered the bones. The Mennonites were thus able to buy the plows they needed and make the land productive. They introduced hard wheat to the United States, and it soon became a common crop on American farms.

## HELPING WORKERS IMPROVE THEIR LIVES

David Dubinsky, a Russian Jewish immigrant, wanted to do something to improve life for other Russian American Jews during those early years. In 1900, he formed the International Ladies Garment Workers' Union, which helped build cooperative, low-cost apartments and established health centers, nurseries, summer camps, and adult education classes. The union is still an important advocate for workers today, with 175,000 members.

peace. Most Jewish Russian immigrants settled in big cities like New York, Philadelphia, and Chicago. They brought little money with them, but they had strong beliefs and a great determination to succeed. Many of them became peddlers; others continued the various crafts they had learned in Russia, and some took jobs in the growing garment industry.

Life was tough for these Russians, too. In the clothing factories, ten or more people would be crowded into one room, making coats, pants, or belts for as long as seventeen hours a day. These rooms were called "sweatshops," because of the close, cramped conditions and intolerable heat, especially in the summer.

Life had its brighter moments, though. There was Friday evening at the synagogue, followed by a traditional meal shared with relatives and neighbors. Russian Jews also spoke Yiddish together, a language similar to German but with Hebrew, Polish, and Russian phrases mixed in, and shared their special foods and talked about the old country.

The younger Jewish Russian immigrants went to American schools, where they learned English, and many went on to become professionals, such as lawyers and teachers. Family ties remained strong, as did concern for any Russian Jews who were especially poverty stricken. They were often helped with loans to get them on their feet.

## Discrimination and the "Red Scare"

The idea of a society in which people were treated equally appealed to some of the Russian immigrants who had left czarist Russia. The leaders of the Russian Revolution promised Russians such a just society in 1917. Although many Russian immigrants wanted nothing to do with the revolutionaries, some of the immigrants had supported them when they were in Russia. Others had become disillusioned with the capitalist system in the United States, which had not led to the good life they had hoped for. Some of these Russian immigrants wanted to return to Russia but were refused permission by the U.S. government.

The government and media had become concerned about possible communist plots in the United States, so between November 1919 and April 1920, three thousand Rus-

These orphans arrived in the United States during the early 1920s. Their parents were among the many members of the Russian nobility who lost their lives during the revolution.

sians suspected of being communists were arrested and jailed. Most were released shortly afterward, but some were sent back to Russia. At the same time, U.S. troops were sent to fight the Red Army in 1920 near the end of the Russian Revolution. (Because their flag was red, communists became known as "Reds" and their army was called the "Red Army.")

The "Red Scare," as it was called, was a period of unreasonable fear of communism that swept the States during this time. As a result, Russian workers were often fired by suspicious employers just because they were Russian. Public hysteria declined eventually, and the brief period of discrimination against Russian Americans came to an end.

## Refugees from the Revolution

When the Russian Revolution started in 1917, a new type of immigrant arrived in the United States. These Russians were also penniless, having abandoned their fortunes in Russia. They also had no trades or work skills, as many of them had never worked in their lives. This was because they were the nobility, who had lived off the work of serfs in Russia for centuries.

They did have social skills, though, so many found work as waiters, maids, and doormen in restaurants and hotels. Some became butlers, cooks, and chauffeurs in wealthy homes. One princess, who had enjoyed doing needlework in Russia, made and sold quilts; an officer in the czar's army

Not all Russians came to the United States penniless. The two women at this ball in New York in 1935 are former members of Russian nobility: a Grand Duchess and a Princess.

opened a riding academy; a prince opened a restaurant in New York. Many middle-class professionals, such as university professors, were also forced to flee the revolution. Most of them learned English and continued their professions in the United States.

## World War II Refugees

Many of the Russian men and women who had been taken as slave labor to the factories in Germany during World War II preferred to go to the United States rather than return home when they were rescued by U.S. troops at the end of the war. While in U.S. refugee camps in Europe, they were matched up with jobs in the States, given medical examinations, and then brought to their new homes throughout the United States. They

were taught to speak English and were quickly assimilated into American culture. It was difficult for these immigrants, most of whom did not settle in large Russian American communities, to preserve their culture.

## Immigration at the End of the Twentieth Century

When the Soviet Union collapsed a few years ago, the new Russian government allowed Russians to emigrate, and the U.S. government allowed them into the country if they could prove they were being persecuted or had relatives already in the States. As a result, possibly a million Russians have moved to the States in recent years. Most of the new arrivals have settled in New York and California and have found some support

## CHANGING THE WAY THEY EAT

An immigrant living in New York says that one difference between life in Russia and life here is the eating habits: "The way we ate in Russia was completely different from the way you Americans eat. We never went out, as there were almost no restaurants and they were too expensive anyway. So we always cooked at home, where we knew the food was prepared properly.

And we never snacked. We had breakfast at home before going to work. We worked, we ate our lunch, we worked some more, and then we went home for dinner. We never stopped for tea breaks or coffee breaks. It's the same for us today in America, except after fifteen years, we go out all the time: We eat at restaurants at least once a week now."

from fellow Russian Americans. Of these recent immigrants, most have been Russian Jews, who have created large communities in Brooklyn and Brighton Beach, New York.

Although many recent arrivals had been professionals, such as accountants, doctors, engineers, and lawyers, in Russia, most have been able to find only less-skilled positions in the United States, such as driving taxis and cleaning offices. To receive their professional licenses in the States, they have to study for and take exams, in addition to learning English well. This can be a formidable barrier for an immigrant who, at the same time, has to keep working to pay the bills.

Although life was hard for Russians when they first arrived in the United States, they worked hard and helped create the land of plenty and freedom that they had sought when they left the repression of their homeland. Those who arrived recently are going through the same process of becoming familiar with their new environment and freedoms, working hard to learn the language and customs, while establishing themselves and making a success of their lives. In the process, life in the Russian American home and community has changed considerably, as immigrants have found throughout the century.

## THEY'RE ONLY SAYING "HELLO!"

Like many continental Europeans, Russian men often greet each other with three kisses on the cheek: first the left side, then the right, then the left cheek again. Some men also kiss a woman's hand on first seeing her. When two Russians meet, one will say in Russian, "Pleased to meet you," and the other will reply, "Very pleas-

ant," meaning that it is very pleasant to see the other person, too.

When they immigrate to the United States, though, most Russians stop practicing these traditional greetings, because they are not considered the normal way to say hello in the States, and Russian Americans prefer not to appear "different" in their behavior.

A Russian bakery in Brighton Beach, Brooklyn, New York.

# CHAPTER THREE

# FAMILY AND COMMUNITY
## A MERGING OF CULTURES

The Russian family traditionally had a strong father figure and a mother who ran the home. The children were expected to be polite and obedient and to study in school or work. This is not so different from families in any Western country during the nineteenth century. Russian Americans were different primarily because they spoke Russian and had their own customs and beliefs.

### As Traditions Slipped Away

Over the generations, many Russian families in the United States let go of the culture that set them apart and became more American. One third-generation Russian American teacher talked of her experience:

"My grandmother brought my mother over in 1921, when she was four years old. They made friends with twenty other families on the boat from Russia, and so all of them settled in the same street. They spoke Russian together and stayed in the same neighborhood for years, even though some moved to different streets later on. As they had no phones or televisions, many hours were spent playing and visiting with friends in their houses. The community made a home-away-from-home for the grownups, and they were all very close.

"My grandmother insisted my mother go to school, including higher education. And that's when the community fell apart,

This Russian American boy and his mother have been browsing through this Russian bookstore in Chicago. The cabinet to his left contains medals and other Russian artifacts.

**These Russian American students face the same challenges in successfully completing their education as other American children. As a group, Russian American children score well academically.**

because the universities the second-generation Russian Americans attended were in different towns. After they graduated, the students like my mother settled in other parts of the country. Although they stayed in touch with family and some friends, their horizons had expanded beyond the old Russian culture of their parents. My grandmother is dead now, but I still remember the stories she used to tell me in her broken English.

"My mother only spoke English to me and passed on very little of the Russian culture. I have passed on none to my children. I have very little contact with other Russian Americans today."

Russians who settled in the United States without the benefit of other Russians nearby lost their culture rapidly. One Russian doctor, who brought her daughter over when she was ten, said that the girl had become Americanized within six months. She had wanted to be as much like her American school friends as possible, and she thought the habits and customs of her parents were peculiar.

This story was repeated by the Russians who came to the United States after World War II. Many of them are still alive today, and their children were brought up with Russian spoken at home. One professor, whose son went to college out of state and married a non-Russian American, talks fondly of how his son recites Russian poems and speaks only Russian on his visits to them. But the son does not speak Russian with his children.

There were three reasons English was spoken to children at home by some Russian American parents: First, it was easier to express ideas based on American culture in English; second, the children had to learn English, not Russian, in order to succeed in the United States; and third, many of the immigrants wanted to become Americans more than they wanted to stay Russian.

## Some Communities Fell Apart

The elders in the Russian communities in the United States tried to maintain the Russian life they knew. But when the younger generations were introduced to American ideas at school, they found they had to make a choice between staying with the old or going with the new. So they left the neighborhoods their parents had created. Their parents wanted them to stay in the communities and help preserve the Russian

traditions that were important to them, but their children, who viewed these neighborhoods as old and depressing, preferred to make their lives a success in American terms, with a house in a "good" neighborhood and a professional career. Although the parents and children remained in touch, they found they had little in common.

There are few of these old, close-knit Russian communities remaining now. The ones that come closest to this kind of community are in San Francisco and Brighton Beach in Brooklyn, New York, where the young and old can live in the same city, even if not in the same neighborhood. There were 110,000 Russian Americans living in San Francisco in 1990, with Russian restaurants and stores throughout the community,

**These Russian Americans enjoy drinks at a Russian restaurant on the boardwalk in Brighton Beach at sunset.**

as well as an annual festival in February offering Russian food, crafts, and entertainment that draws the community together.

## Russian Families That Kept Their Culture

Although Russian culture has eroded over time in many communities and families, many Russian American families have maintained their customs and language through their close connection to their church. They regularly say prayers at home and go to church services together. They send their children to Sunday school and speak Russian at home. When sons marry, they are expected to settle nearby, so that the families and communities can remain together.

These families have either kept or adapted the customs of their ancestors, such as keeping elderly parents at home. Another custom is giving birth at home, if possible, so that friends and family can celebrate immediately after the baby's birth. Traditionally, everyone goes to the house after the birth, eats dinner, and toasts the parents and newborn child with drinks and songs, lavishing the baby with money or gifts.

## The Changing Role of Women

During the first wave of immigration prior to 1910, only one in every fifty adult Russian immigrants was a woman. There were so few that when one young woman put an advertisement in a Russian-language newspaper for a secretarial position, within a week she received over fifty replies asking for her hand in marriage!

One way some women earned an income for their families was by renting rooms in their apartments and looking after

**Wearing a fur collar and hat that are characteristically Russian, this mother keeps warm while walking with her daughter on a windy day.**

the lodgers. Unmarried Russian American men either shared apartments and ate at restaurants or rented rooms in boarding houses where Russian American women cooked for them and washed their clothes.

Other women earned money by working in factories making candy or cloth. Women in mining towns supplemented the family income by raising chickens and selling the eggs. Others helped run family farms. Few of these women had much money after rent, food, and other necessities were paid for. There were no luxuries like pretty dresses and lipstick; some of the women did not even have shoes. Their work was long and hard, and being pregnant was considered no reason to stay away from work. A pregnant woman would stop heavy work only a short while before giving birth and would be back on the job soon afterward. Although the next generation made sure its children were educated, the girls only went through high school; they were expected to marry and become housewives by the time they were eighteen.

Life for Russian American women today is a far cry from the life their mothers and grandmothers knew. Third- and fourth-generation Russian American women grew up with the English language and American culture, completed their education, and

The brightly colored clothes outside this woman's store in the East Village, New York City, have the same lively appeal as those of her homeland.

became part of America's army of working women.

## Education in Two Cultures

For Russian American children, life has also changed in many ways. Early Russian immigrants at the turn of the twentieth century followed the same pattern as their parents, putting their children to work after a few years of school. Most of the children left school around seventh grade to help support

These girls, the children of Russian Jewish immigrants, attend a school for Jewish girls in Brooklyn. The Jewish American community has long welcomed Soviet and Russian Jewish emigrés into its ranks.

the family and barely knew how to read or write. Teenage boys became office or messenger boys, drivers, clerks, or factory workers. The girls went to work in clothing stores or factories. Even so, these children already knew English better than Russian and often answered in English when their parents spoke to them in Russian.

When those first immigrant children grew up, they wanted to educate their own children. They knew that getting a good education was the best way to succeed financially in the United States and get better jobs than working in factories or mines. As a result, those second-generation Russian Americans did become educated. In fact, most Russian American children have done very well at school, many of them going on to college.

Parents who wanted their children educated in Russian culture and religion as well as in the U.S. school system sent their children to Sunday schools run by the Russian Orthodox Church in Exile in areas where there were enough children to enroll. To this day, these schools have been the most effective way of preserving Russian culture in the States. Russian language, literature, geography, music, dance, and religion are taught for one or two days a week. Most of the students do not like all the extra study or homework, but they are rewarded for their hard work when they look back at the strong sense of identity the schooling has given them.

From the point of view of preserving Russian culture in the United States, these schools have an added benefit. Because they have so much in common, the students spend much of their free time together and often marry each other. Their children are therefore brought up speaking Russian and belonging to the Russian Orthodox Church.

For families not connected with the Russian Orthodox Church in Exile, there are few ways of formally teaching the culture to their children. Many parents speak Russian to their children, give them books about Russia, and tell them stories about Russia. Arranging trips to Russia so they can see the culture for themselves is probably the best way to acquaint children with their heritage and is now much easier to do since the fall of the Soviet Union.

### Dating and Marriage

A more interesting subject to most young people than school is dating, for which Russian Americans have long had their own rules based on their own traditions.

Early Russian immigrant boys and girls had a difficult time dating each other. The girls were chaperoned when they went to the movies or community activities, such as dances at the parish hall and picnics in the city park. On the other hand, the boys were expected to chase girls, as long as they were not Russian. Their fathers would tell them, "Go enjoy yourself, but stay away from the Russian girls. Be quiet about it and be careful." They wanted their own daughters to marry without dating.

The preferred way for a Russian boy and girl to meet was through matchmaking. Two mothers would get together and arrange

## MARRIAGE IN THE CHURCH

In Russia, the Russian Orthodox Church was, by law, the only religion in which any Russian could be married. That law does not exist in the United States, but the U.S. Russian Orthodox Church will allow a couple to marry in the Orthodox Church today only if they are both members of the Church. One Russian American couple in New York with four children allowed them to date anyone they wanted. But they encouraged them to marry only Russian Orthodox men or women. They had no trouble until the last daughter wanted to marry an American Indian. The parents agreed to the marriage, as long as the man learned Russian and became a Russian Orthodox church member. The man agreed, and the couple's children speak Russian and attend church with their parents.

for their children to meet at a community dance or festival. The boy's mother would suggest just before the event that he take the girl home after the dance. But then the parents would walk with them. If they were attracted to each other, the boy and girl would continue to meet with a chaperone present. After about half a year, he would give her an engagement ring if they wanted to marry.

The girl's parents would then celebrate with a party that was similar to an American bridal shower. The girl's mother would give her a set of bedding. The boy's parents contributed glassware or dishes, and other relatives would give money and other gifts. The wedding would take place a month or two later.

These Russian veterans fought in the Soviet Army as allies of the United States during World War II. They later emigrated to the United States and have kept in touch with each other ever since.

is mainly a lobbying organization with thirty state chapters around the United States. It also occasionally promotes Russian culture by showing Russian movies and sponsoring concerts, as well as providing a meeting ground for Russians in the States.

A few social clubs have been organized by different Russian communities around the country, such as the Russian American Club in St. Petersburg, Florida. The members are all immigrants who came to the the United States after World War II and have now retired. The club gives them an opportunity to meet and celebrate the way they are used to, with traditional songs, poetry readings, lectures, and plays, all in the Russian language. Once a year, members dress up in traditional costumes and dance together.

## Russian American Societies

No central organization has been established in the United States specifically to preserve Russian culture. The Congress of Russian Americans was formed in 1973 to protect the rights of the Russian minority in this country. It also tries to correct the false idea that all Russians are communists and that Russian culture is the same as Soviet culture. The Congress of Russian Americans

## Holding On to What Is Russian

Most Russians in the United States keep in touch with their homeland from afar. Although some of them enjoy visits to Russia, the majority stay in the States and listen to records of Russian music or read books and newspapers in order to find out about their culture and motherland. When the Red Star Army Chorus and Dance Ensemble or the Bolshoi Ballet tours the United States, it is safe to assume that many Russian Americans will be in the audience.

Although the owner of this delicatessen speaks only Russian, the shops signs are in Russian, and the food sold here is Russian, the shop is in Chicago.

Russian Americans have a great interest in their homeland, although they feel strongly about the way the Soviet government tried to destroy their churches, religion, customs, and traditions. And so, whenever the opportunity arises, they find out more about what was good and grand in the Russian culture from the time of the czars. One group organized an American tour of the treasures of the czars, and this caused great excitement among Russians here.

## Russian Americans in the Workplace

Russian Americans have not specialized in any particular type of business, but many of them have become highly trained scientists and professionals. A survey in the 1970s showed that Russian American families had the highest income level of all the major ethnic groups in the United States, and many of those working were professionals.

### BANKS THAT HELP

Unlike the banks that took advantage of Russian immigrants eighty years ago, U.S. banks today have helped recent arrivals manage their money. One bank cooperated with a local group in New York to educate new Russian immigrants on how to use banks and has even installed Russian-language ATMs (automated teller machines) in the city.

## Russian American Newspapers

In the 1970s, one-third of a million Americans spoke Russian as their first language. They had two dozen Russian-language newspapers and magazines to choose from, with a combined circulation of sixty-five thousand copies each week.

Today, there are two national daily Russian-language newspapers in the States. One of them, *Russkava Zhizn* (pronounced "SHEE-zen" and meaning "Russian Life"), is printed in San Francisco. The other is *Novoye Russkoye Slovo* ("New Russian Word"), which has been printed in New York since 1910. It is the oldest continually running Russian-language newspaper in the world. The paper has a circulation of thirty thousand and is read all over the world. Even Boris Yeltsin, the president of Russia, says he reads it.

Because both of these newspapers are written in Russian, it is mainly the older, first-generation Russian Americans who read and understand them. Some articles in these papers mention the lack of interest younger generations show in their Russian language and roots, as they rapidly become involved in modern American culture.

## Russians and U.S. Politics

Whatever their political preferences in the United States, the Russians who have come to live here speak highly of the political freedom they find. Some say that they are not sent to prison camps in Alaska for telling a neighbor that the Democrats do more for the country than Republicans. None of them have been arrested yet, their property confiscate, or children killed, for attending a political convention. They can hold meetings in their homes without worrying about who is spying on them for the secret police.

This Russian immigrant, who runs a Russian book and art store in Chicago, takes time out to catch up on the daily news from one of his shop's Russian-language newspapers.

## ORGANIZED CRIME, RUSSIAN STYLE

Unlike earlier generations of Russian immigrants who were generally law abiding, a few criminal gangs have come to North America from Russia in the last decade. What some call the Russian Mafia, or *Organizatsiya,* has been busy in New York and California and has become involved in health insurance fraud, counterfeiting, murder, and even the sale of nuclear weapons.

One gang in California copied people's credit card numbers to make fake credit cards. They then used them to buy gas, filling huge gas tanks they had had custom built in their cars. Next, the gas was transferred into tanks at their own gas stations and sold to regular customers. Like many criminals, these gang members were eventually caught.

Although there is no Russian political organization in the United States. Russian Americans here are very interested in politics. They will spend many hours talking about events in Russia, the United States, and the rest of the world. They are especially interested in their homeland, and most of them want President Yeltsin's plans for a better life for Russians to work.

## Discrimination

The only significant prejudice against Russians in the United States occurred during the Red Scare between 1919 and 1920, at a time when most immigrants of all nationalities were unpopular. Russian Americans lost their jobs simply because they were Russian, and some Russians were even jailed for a brief time.

Many Russian Americans were scared at that time of being deported back to a country where they would certainly face death for having left, and they did everything they could to become American. They learned to speak English and tried to disconnect from the things that identified them as Russian. One old man, who had a beautiful library of Russian books, burned them to avoid being viewed as a communist. And that was the

problem: Although almost no Russian immigrants were communists, many Americans at the time thought all Russians were communists and therefore a possible enemy. This idea changed in later years with regard to Russians living in the the United States. During the Cold War, when the Soviet Union was the enemy of the United States, individual Russians living in America were not discriminated against. They had not only assimilated well, but were also opposed to the Soviet government.

Russian immigrants today are generally the subject of interest to Americans rather than of discrimination. After so many years of being cut off from Russia, more Americans have come face to face with Russian immigrants and developed a fascination with the country and culture left behind.

In the same way that Russians have been free to go about their own lives as individuals in the United States, they have also been free to practice their own religion, whether it be Russian Orthodox, Catholic, Protestant, Jewish, or Islamic. After decades and even centuries of religious persecution in Russia and later the Soviet Union, this must present quite a difference for each immigrant as he or she settles into life in the United States.

Holy Trinity Cathedral, a Chicago landmark. The local Russian community hired an American architect to design this church in a style that would remind them of rural southern Russia.

# CHAPTER FOUR

# RELIGION AND CELEBRATIONS
## THE SPIRITUAL RUSSIANS

Although there are many religions in Russia, most ethnic Russians belong to the Russian Orthodox Church. The Church traces its beginnings to the birth of Christianity. Christians belonged to one Church until it separated in A.D. 1054 into the Roman Catholic Church, based in Rome, and the Eastern Orthodox Church, based in Constantinople (now called Istanbul) in Turkey.

Although the two churches are very similar, the main difference is that the Eastern Orthodox Church follows strictly the original writings of the early Church, which is why it is called "Orthodox." Eastern Orthodox prayers today are the same as the ones said nearly two thousand years ago. The Russian Orthodox Church is one of several national branches of the Eastern Orthodox Church. The Russian Orthodox Church separated from the Eastern Orthodox Church in 1453, when Constantinople was taken over by Muslims.

The Russian Orthodox Church has close ties with the Greek Orthodox Church. In fact, the name of the Russian Orthodox Church in the United States used to be the Russian Orthodox Greek Catholic Church of America. Although each has strong national interests, there has been talk of recombining both Orthodox religions into one Orthodox Church as it used to be 550 years ago.

### Two Russian Orthodox Churches

The Russian Orthodox Church came to North America two hundred years ago through Alaska and is the Church most Russian Americans have attended since then. It is now called the Orthodox Church in North America. St. Nicholas Church, the

### BISHOP VENIAMINOV AND THE ALEUT

The first Russian Orthodox bishop in Russian Alaska was Veniaminov, who was appointed in 1814. He lived in the Aleutian Islands for many years with his family and reportedly converted all the Aleuts in his area (estimated at twelve thousand by 1850) to Christianity. He did not force them to become Christians but helped them modernize their culture. Veniaminov wrote a dictionary, grammar book, and primer in the Aleut language and taught the Aleuts to read. He recorded their legends and folklore and studied the winds, tides, plant life, wildlife, rocks, and soil on all the islands where he preached. He had a cathedral built in New Archangel (Sitka) and trained some Aleuts as priests to minister to the Native Alaskans. By 1861, nine Russian Orthodox churches and thirty-five chapels had been built in Alaska.

This Russian Orthodox log church in Eklutna, a small village outside Anchorage, Alaska, is very much in use today. The church combines Russian and Native American influences, resulting in such features as gravestones that are small, brightly colored doll houses for the spirits of the dead to live in.

## THE SUPPRESSION OF RELIGION IN THE SOVIET UNION

At the time of the Russian Revolution in 1917, there were eighty thousand Russian Orthodox churches and chapels and six thousand synagogues in the country. By the time the Soviet government finally fell apart seventy years later, and following decades of religious persecution and the killing of many priests, rabbis, and their families, there were only seven thousand Russian Orthodox churches and one hundred synagogues in use, all of them under government control.

oldest Russian Orthodox church in the United States, was built in 1792 near Anchorage, Alaska.

After World War II, another Russian Orthodox Church came to the States. This one, which is called the Russian Orthodox Church in Exile, had actually started in what was then Yugoslavia in 1922. The bishops of the Russian Orthodox Church were instructed by the head of the Russian Orthodox Church in Moscow to set up their own Church outside Russia, just before he was murdered by the Soviet government.

Both Russian Orthodox Churches have the same beliefs. The only difference between the two, apart from each having its own bishops, priests, and church buildings, is that the Russian Orthodox Church in Exile uses only Russian in its services and refuses to have anything to do with the Church in Russia, which it distrusts because of its long association with the Soviet government.

Although some Russian Americans go to both churches today, many stay with the Russian Orthodox Church in America because they can understand the English services. The Russian Orthodox Church in Exile has perhaps one hundred thousand members, most of whom used to live in Russia and grew up speaking the language. Either they came over shortly after World War II and are now retired or they are Russians who immigrated recently. Many of these first-generation Russian Americans still speak only Russian, and thus they prefer the Russian services.

## Church and Community Growing Together

As Russian communities formed, they built their own churches. It was not long before a cathedral was built in San Francisco

## THE OLD BELIEVERS

There is actually a third Russian Orthodox Church in the States. The "Old Believers" follow the teachings of the Russian Orthodox Church before they were changed slightly in 1654. There are only a few of them living around the world today. They were persecuted in Russia and moved to other countries, including China.

After World War II, Old Believers in China were told by the government there that they could not practice their religion, and so they moved to Oregon during the 1960s. Although they lived in isolated communities, they found that the Western world was beginning to influence their younger members and take them away from their strict beliefs. They moved north to Alaska and settled in four truly isolated communities there. The children are taught in Russian, wear seventeenth-century clothes, and have very little contact with American society.

in 1881, and the Russian Orthodox Church in America was run from there. In 1905, as more Russians arrived in New York, the headquarters was moved to New York City, where it still remains. By 1916, there were 170 Russian Orthodox churches in America, with almost a hundred thousand members. The churches also ran 126 religious education schools (on Saturdays or during the week after regular school hours), with 150 teachers and nearly 7,000 students.

The church benefited its community in ways beyond offering spiritual guidance and worship services. The church helped establish societies (such as the Russian Orthodox Catholic Women's Mutual Aid Society, founded in 1907 in Pittsburgh, Pennsylvania) to help spread the faith, as well as assist Russian Americans who might be injured at work. A missionary school was opened in Minneapolis, Minnesota, in 1898 to train new priests and translate religious books into English.

The Church recognized that Russian Americans were losing touch with their language and that they needed not only books in English but religious services as well, so they could understand them. The Church continued to be a vital part of Russian American communities and today has perhaps as many as one million members and 350 churches.

## Russian American Churches Today

Today, language is a concern in both Russian Orthodox denominations. Russian-

This bishop is holding a Bible class for the children of Russian immigrants on a farm in 1944. The woman to his right is Alexandra Tolstoy, daughter of the famous Russian author Leo Tolstoy.

speaking churches are the main institution preserving the Russian language in the United States. Few second-, third-, and fourth-generation Russian Americans who attend the Russian Orthodox Church in America, where services are conducted in English, speak Russian. Some of them have attended religious education programs, and some have spoken Russian at home, but the majority do not know the language.

The Russian Orthodox Church in Exile has tried to introduce English services in its churches as well, in order to attract more Russian Americans to church, but there is resistance to this idea from the traditional members of the congregations. The feeling among older Russian Americans is that once the language is lost, most of the cultural heritage is also lost. Although this may appear to be a good reason to have services in Russian, the insistence on speaking Russian has resulted in many members leaving the Church because they cannot understand the service.

Despite this debate over language in the Church in Exile, both churches act as the focal point, or center, of Russian communities in the United States. Apart from a few clubs set up in some communities, the occasional performance of Russian folk dances or music, and a couple of national daily newspapers, nothing else brings Russian Americans together in the way that the church does.

The Church was a central part of life in Russia for centuries and even defined what a Russian was. Even today, many ethnic Russians do not consider someone to be Russian unless he or she is a member of the Russian Orthodox Church. Even Russian Americans who do not go to church feel strongly about the importance of the Church in keeping Russian traditions. For this reason, Russian Americans usually try to introduce their children to the church and make them participate in religious education wherever possible so that they will have some sense of their roots and heritage.

## Religious Holidays, Celebrations, and Forms of Worship

Russians were converted to Russian Orthodoxy a thousand years ago because the czar was so impressed by the services of the Eastern Orthodox Church. He had decided to find a suitable religion for his country and sent envoys around Europe and the Middle East. Their mission was to visit the centers of the major religions of the time and learn about each one. When they arrived at the Eastern Orthodox Church in Constantinople and attended the services, they thought they had gone to heaven. The czar was equally impressed with the beauty and ceremony of Orthodox rites, and he ordered his fellow Russians to become Christians.

In the United States, the Russian Orthodox Church has its own religious festivals and shares many with other Christian denominations. It has also adopted the American holiday of Thanksgiving, which gives Russian Americans a chance to celebrate an American holiday using customs and traditions from both cultures.

**Easter.** Easter is considered the most important religious holiday because it is the time Jesus is believed to have arisen from the dead. For the Orthodox Church, it is a happy time spent with close friends and family. On the day

before Easter, colored eggs are made and exchanged with friends after breakfast as a symbol of good luck. During the day, baskets of food, fruit, and more colored eggs are prepared by the women. At eleven at night, the congregation meets at the church, and women place the baskets in a circle to be blessed by the priest.

A bishop blesses baskets of food just before the midnight Easter service. In his right hand, he is swinging the censer that holds burning incense.

51

This icon, like other Russian Orthodox icons, conforms to certain rules dictating acceptable subjects and artistic methods.

## THE SIGN OF THE CROSS

When the Orthodox Russians cross themselves, they place the thumb and next two fingers together, with the last two fingers against the palm, and touch their forehead, chest, and both shoulders. The three fingers held together represent God, Jesus, and the Holy Spirit and the places they touch mean that they will use their mind, soul, and strength to do what God, Jesus, and the Holy Spirit expect them to do.

The service begins at 11:30 at night, and at midnight, the traditional procession around the church takes place. This procession symbolizes the search for the body of Jesus after he rose from the dead. Traditionally, fireworks are set off to symbolize Jesus ascending to heaven and to show the happy holiday spirit of the members. These early Easter morning services last between three and five hours, depending on the congregation's stamina.

**The Eucharist.** The most important regular rite in the Orthodox Church is the Eucharist, or communion service. The Eucharist is a special service for church members to celebrate Jesus' last meal. It is usually held in the morning, and the faithful may not eat after midnight of the night before. Before the service begins, they also must go to confession and seek forgiveness for their recent sins. During the service, prayers are said and each person goes to the front of the church to eat a small wafer that has been dipped in a cup of wine passed around by the priest. The wafer and wine represent the body and blood of Jesus himself, as well as the bread and wine that Jesus consumed during his last meal with his followers. In all Russian Orthodox services, the congregation sings without the accompaniment of musical instruments. This gives their services an especially traditional quality.

**Icons.** Icons play an important part in Russian Orthodox religious life. Icons are paintings, usually on wood, that tell the story of Jesus, his mother Mary, the saints, and stories from the Bible. The word *icon* comes from the Greek word for image or picture. Icons were used for centuries to tell religious stories to people who could not read. The pictures range in size from six feet high to only an inch and are kept at home and in churches, carried into battle, and made into necklaces that can be worn all the time. Icons themselves are not worshiped, but they help the faithful pray by providing an image of whom they are praying to.

In churches and homes, Russians will light a beeswax candle and place it under an icon. They kneel before it, make the traditional sign of the cross, and pray. They also kiss or touch their forehead against the icon and sometimes smother it in incense (a fragrant smoke). People or icons are sometimes honored by being covered with incense from a censer ( a metal container that is filled with burning incense and swung from a chain). Icons do not have to be fancy or expensive to be treated with great respect and reverence. They merely have to be blessed by a priest who sprinkles holy water over them; even a photograph of an old icon can be used for this purpose.

Like some other Christian churches, Russian Orthodox churches are built in the shape of a cross. Everything in the church is placed according to tradition. On the left, for instance, is a large wooden crucifix with an icon of Jesus. The faithful place candles in front of the icon in memory of dead friends or relatives. Between the altar and the congregation is a wooden screen with specific icons on it, behind which only priests are allowed.

These women are carrying icons of Jesus during a celebration on Easter Sunday in New York.

**Fasting.** Fasting is a regular part of the Russian Orthodox calendar. Like many religions, the Church encourages its members to give up certain favorite foods and concentrate on their spiritual lives during certain parts of the year. In fact, fasting is a regular practice for Orthodox Russians. Every Wednesday and Friday is a fast day, and there are ten other fasts during the year, varying in length from one day to almost two months just before Christmas. When Orthodox Russians fast, they avoid all animal products, which means no meat, fish, milk, cheese, or eggs. They are allowed to eat fruit, vegetables, grains, and beans. As one of the priests said to his parishioners, "Fasting is even good for your health."

## Baptisms, Weddings, and Funerals

As with most Christian churches, Russian Orthodoxy considers baptism an impor-

Although this bride and groom are dressed in Western wedding clothes, they still wear the Russian crowns that signify their rule as king and queen of their own household.

starts without the bride and groom, as the congregation takes the Eucharist. The bride and bridegroom then walk into the church and stand in the middle of the aisle. The priest places rings on their right hands. Songs are chanted during much of the service, one of which reminds the couple of a traditional — if somewhat old-fashioned — family arrangement: "The man is the head of the household and the woman must follow him."

After prayers are said, the couple tie themselves together with a rope from the priest's robe, and the priest puts a white cloth over their hands showing that no one can untie the bond being created. He then covers their heads with part of his robes, showing that they will be protected from evil. The couple is formally married when the priest places crowns on their heads, signifying that they are king and queen in their own family. After the couple drinks from the same cup of wine three times (signifying the Holy Trinity of God, Jesus, and the Holy Spirit), the priest leads them around the church three times, and the choir sings a song, wishing them many years of happiness. The couple kiss and make the sign of the cross over each other, and the wedding ceremony is over.

The last church ceremony in a person's earthly existence is the funeral. Russian Orthodox funerals are much the same as in other religions, except that cremations are forbidden. Every year, on the anniversary of

tant stage in a person's life. The Russian Orthodox Church baptizes infants by dipping them three times into water and then giving them a cross to wear. They then become official members of the Russian Orthodox Church.

Another important event in life is marriage. Wedding ceremonies are always happy occasions, but they are especially so in the Russian Orthodox Church. The service a family member's death, the Russian community expects the family to hold a special service, called a requiem, in honor of the person who died. It is a way for the community, as well as the family, to remember that person.

## Jews and Mennonites

Other religions followed by some Russians in the United States are primarily the Jewish and Mennonite faiths. Russian Jews who attend synagogues usually join congregations already established by Jews in their own areas. They do not form their own congregations or practice their faith as a distinctly Russian one. Like most American Jews, they strive to become members not only of their Jewish community but of the community at large.

The Mennonites are a denomination of Anabaptist Protestants who believe in nonviolence. Some dress plainly, like the Amish, and live very simply, but others have adopted a modern way of life. Mennonites do not baptize infants, encouraging people instead to join the church when they are old enough to make up their own minds. Conservative Mennonites also expect members to marry other members and oppose holding public office and taking oaths.

Whatever their religion, whichever group they belonged to, and whenever they emigrated, there is one thing that most Russian Americans love to do, and that is get together with their friends and have a good time dancing, singing, and drinking. These are opportunities to forget all the pressures and troubles in their lives and just let their Russian spirits loose.

## FAITH HEALINGS AND SUPERSTITIONS

Russians have traditionally used faith healers to try to cure any illness or problem a person might have. These faith healers use herbs, roots, tree bark, flowers, and plants, in combination with prayer, to heal or at least to make a person feel better.

Russians also used to believe in such superstitious rituals as never stepping over a child for fear of stunting his or her growth. People who caught themselves gossiping were supposed to say "Poo-poo" and spit three times in order to clear their minds of the bad thoughts.

As a family member grieves over the loss of her loved one, a priest blesses the grave by swinging a censer.

55

A folk dancer, dressed in the rich costume of her homeland, entertains New Yorkers at an open-air theater with a dance called "Bylba."

# CHAPTER FIVE

# CUSTOMS, EXPRESSIONS, AND HOSPITALITY
## THE FRIENDLY RUSSIANS

**W**hen her husband died, one Russian American woman spent lots of money throwing the wildest party she could afford after the burial service. Was she glad to see him go? No, she was simply following the Russian tradition of giving the deceased one last party with all his or her friends. Today, most Russian Americans settle for simple dinner parties. But some, like the woman in this story, still send off friends and relatives in the traditional Russian way, with a big celebration.

In a way, her story is typical of the way Russians live their lives — finding something to cheer them, even in the face of tragedy. Most Russians are gregarious, which is to say, they like to spend time together talking, telling stories, singing, and laughing. Although they need no special reason to celebrate together, a few traditional occasions still call for parties, and perhaps the wedding is the best known of these.

### Traditional Celebrations Today

Weddings are the grandest of Russian celebrations, with feasting and drinking sometimes lasting up to three days, as was traditional in Russia. Not all customs are followed in all weddings today, but most employ some traditional elements, making Russian American weddings unique and joyous occasions.

The wedding day might start with a small orchestra playing at the bride's house at eight in the morning. The bride asks for her parents' blessing of the wedding and then starts to dress with the help of female relatives. Her mother attaches a treasured object, such as an old coin, to her daughter's dress for good luck and then gives her some traditional motherly advice: "The husband is meant to be the person in charge of the family, but a clever woman has many ways of getting her own way."

The relatives then go to church, and the couple follows a short while later. After the wedding service, the family returns home for a wedding breakfast. When the bride and groom arrive, they are given bread to show that they will never be hungry. Pictures are taken after breakfast, and then everyone goes to a large hall, where a banquet of food and drink awaits them.

The bride and groom greet the guests as they enter the hall, and the guests, in turn, drink a glass of whiskey to wish the couple good luck. After kissing the bride, the guests are escorted by the bridesmaids to their tables. The meal begins at six in the evening, with the bridesmaids serving the food. A band plays Russian music until ten o'clock, when it's time to follow an elaborate Russian ritual for collecting money for the newlyweds.

The bride and groom join the revelry at their wedding reception. Celebrations like this capture a feeling of enthusiasm and the love of a good time that are equally Russian and American.

First, the bride and groom move to a central table with their mothers while the band plays the wedding march. Then, each guest comes to the table and places money in a basket. The lights are turned down so no one can see how much everyone else gives. Then guests kiss the bride and groom and receive a piece of wedding cake. It is customary for unmarried people to take their cake home and place it under their pillows for good luck.

Next comes a game called *"Kot and Mish,"* which means cat and mouse. The groom is the cat and the bride the mouse. Guests form a circle around the bride, and the cat tries to break through and get to the mouse. The guests tease the groom, telling him that if he does not break through the line, he won't be able to sleep with his bride that night. It is hard for the cat to reach the mouse, but usually someone lets him through in the end.

Then, the guests form another circle and the bride takes off her veil. She performs a dance, and people again donate money. This money is meant for the bride to use to prepare for being a mother and to provide for her children when they grow up.

The drinking and dancing continue until one or two in the morning and sometimes as late as dawn. The young couple leaves earlier, and their friends make a game of trying to find them and stop them from going to bed.

The next day, the guests start eating and drinking again in the afternoon and keep going until well past midnight. At eight in the evening, the bride and groom join their guests for dinner. But their friends have a better idea. They take the couple to a cemetery and tie them to different tombstones. They are left there, and they must untie themselves and make their way back to the hall for the rest of the party.

## A TRADITIONAL WELCOME

The Russian sense of hospitality is legendary, perhaps the result of people living so far apart in a vast country. One custom that still exists in some Russian American households is welcoming guests to the house by placing a loaf of bread on a specially carved wooden dish covered with an embroidered towel. A small, matching bowl of salt is placed on top of the loaf. This custom is also used at weddings and for people who have just moved into a new house. It is meant to assure that they will never be short of food.

## Holiday Celebrations

Holidays of all types are welcomed by Russian Americans as opportunities for family and friends to get together. Christmas is one of the most festive, with the main celebrations held on Christmas Eve. Traditionally, people drop in uninvited to wish each other a merry Christmas. In the evening, families pile straw on a table and put a doll representing the baby Jesus on top. After prayers, they clear the table and the adults exchange small gifts, such as alcoholic drinks, clothing, or religious objects. The presents are not expensive, but they are meant as signs of affection. The children have to wait until Christmas Day to receive their presents from St. Nicholas, or Grandfather Frost, as he is also called.

Everyone then eats a large dinner and drinks many toasts for good luck. During the Christmas Eve meal, a crisp bread called *aplotki* is blessed, then broken and passed around the table for people to help themselves to. After the meal, the guests talk and sing their favorite Russian songs, such as "*Katjusha*" and "Carol of the Bells."

One custom followed in close communities of first-generation Russian Americans was for a man dressed as St. Joseph (or a woman dressed as the Virgin Mary) to ring the doorbell at some point during the evening. The visitor would sing two or three Christmas carols and in return receive a glass of whiskey and wishes for a merry Christmas. Sometimes a small amount of money was also given to the visitor, who was usually an important member of the community.

## Easter

*Blini* is the name given to small, light pancakes served with melted butter, sour cream, and other garnishes for which Russians are famous. Blini also refers to the first Sunday in the Lenten season, when these pancakes are made. Traditionally, Russian American women meet in each other's homes in the morning and make different kinds of bread, cheese dishes, and potato pancakes. Following a church service, the food is served for dinner by children in traditional costumes, and a few songs are sung afterward. Today, the custom of making and sharing blini at the beginning of the Lenten fast is falling away in many communities.

At the end of Lent, in the early hours of Easter morning after the service, everyone returns home for breakfast with the baskets of food they took to church to be blessed. To bring good luck, they eat the colored eggs first. Vodka toasts are proposed throughout breakfast, and everyone has a good time. It is forbidden to complain about anything

**The Easter service is almost over, and the families are getting ready to take their baskets home and enjoy a hearty breakfast together.**

during Easter, as it is a time of goodwill and happiness.

### New Year's Eve

Russians have their own way of celebrating New Year's Eve in the United States. Family and friends usually gather at someone's house at eight in the evening. The women bring food. An initial toast is drunk to the New Year, and the guests play several games.

As in the Christmas tradition, a well-known person in the community may go from house to house dressed as an old beggar, wearing tattered clothes and a large false nose with glasses. Sometimes this person is accompanied by a child dressed as the "New Year." When the door opens, the adult says, "Please help a poor soul" and trades jokes with the guests for a few minutes. The beggar continues to beg, asking for money, food, and drink and is finally given a glass of whiskey so he or she can share a toast to the New Year. Although this custom is rarely observed in Russian American communities as a whole now, it is still sometimes practiced among friends.

## FABULOUS EGGS BY FABERGÉ

The colored eggs that Russians traditionally eat at Easter gave rise to a short-lived tradition in the Russian royal court a century ago. From 1885 until the 1917 Russian Revolution, a Russian goldsmith, Peter Carl Fabergé, and his employees made Easter eggs for the Russian royal family. These eggs were not boiled, and they did not come from chickens. They were made with gold, silver, jewels, and other precious stones, and each one took a year to make. There were miniature paintings on the outside, and the tops of the eggs opened to reveal a surprise. One egg had the map of the new Trans-Siberian railway engraved on the outside. Inside was a golden railroad engine, made exactly to scale, with crystals for windows and a ruby for the headlight.

A baker prepares pastries in a Russian bakery in Brighton Beach, New York.

## Traditional Food and Drink

The Russians brought many recipes with them to the United States, such as chicken Kiev (deep-fried, battered chicken breast stuffed with butter and herbs), *shasalik* (lamb with such vegetables as tomatoes, potatoes, and spicy carrots grilled on a stick), and beef stroganoff (thin slices of beef in a sour cream sauce). Sour cream is another Russian specialty that has found its way into the American refrigerator as well as onto the Russian American dinner table.

Borscht, or beet soup, is another favorite. In Russia, beets were an important crop, and so naturally the Russians became experts at making tasty meals with them.

The same goes for cabbage, which they found many ways of cooking. One common dish is cabbage soup. Another is *piroshki*, a crusted pie with either cabbage or beef inside, flavored with onion, dill, salt, and parsley. Russian cooks make cabbage rolls by stuffing cabbage leaves with ground beef and gently stewing them in tomato sauce with potatoes and carrots.

Russians were not able to grow wheat in northern Russia and so grew rye instead. The bread they made from this grain is still eaten as pumpernickel today.

If there is one great Russian contribution to American cuisine, it is bagels and the lox (smoked salmon) they are often served with. Although bagels were popularized by Jews from Russia and other parts of Eastern Europe, they are really Russian in origin. The Russians have eaten bagels (or *bublichki*, as they call them) for a long time in many flavors and sizes; some are so hard that they have to be dunked in tea to soften them before eating. They used to be sold hot on Russian streets during the winter to warm up passersby, in the same way that hot chestnuts can still be bought in some towns in Europe or in New York City.

Russian Americans still eat a few of the popular Russian desserts, such as blini stuffed with fruit, jam, or cream cheese fillings, and *kissel,* which is a thin cranberry jelly drunk as a dessert. At Easter, Russians traditionally eat *pasha koolich,* a rich, log-shaped cake made with cream cheese.

Russians are well known for their tea drinking habits, but most Russian Ameri-

cans have switched to coffee as their hot drink of choice. The ones who do still drink tea continue the southern Russian tradition of adding a slice of lemon to the cup or of using jam, jelly, or honey, which may be added to the tea instead of sugar or eaten with a small spoon as the tea is drunk. Tea is traditionally drunk from a glass placed in a holder with a handle, rather than from a cup.

Another traditional Russian drink that is still very popular with Russian Americans is vodka, an alcoholic drink that looks like water. The word *vodka* actually comes from the Russian word for water *(voda).*

**Bakeries and delis provide Russian immigrants with their favorite foods from home and help them make a smooth transition to their new life in the United States. This deli offers pastries, candies, and other types of food, including canned specialty foods.**

## A RECIPE FOR BEEF STROGANOFF

**Ingredients:**

1 pound fettuccine pasta
2 tablespoons olive oil
1 onion, finely chopped
1 pound mushrooms, sliced
1 pound beef, thinly sliced
2 tablespoons unbleached flour

1 cup beef stock
1 cup milk
1 teaspoon Dijon mustard
1/4 teaspoon pepper
1/2 teaspoon salt
1 cup sour cream

**Directions:**

1. Boil water for pasta and cook pasta according to directions.
2. Heat half the oil in skillet, add onion, and sauté three minutes.
3. Set onions aside and sauté mushrooms in remaining oil for two minutes.
4. Add beef and onions to the skillet and sauté another minute.
5. Sprinkle with flour and stir until absorbed. Slowly add stock and stir for three to five minutes, until thickened.
6. Stir in milk, mustard, and pepper and simmer until thickened, about ten minutes. Remove from heat.
7. In a bowl, whisk salt into sour cream and stir into the stroganoff.
8. Place fettucine on a plate and top with stroganoff.

Serves four.

## What Makes Russians Laugh?

First-generation Russian Americans still laugh at Russian jokes. But their second-generation children find it hard to relate to the Russian sense of humor. Instead, they prefer American jokes.

Russian humor is really the Russians laughing about the misfortunes they had to face in Russia. With all the tough and ridiculous situations they experienced year after year, there was almost nothing else they could do but laugh. For instance, Russians were not very happy with Soviet President Gorbachev's reforms in the 1980s because it was very difficult to get jobs or buy anything in the stores. The Russians also believed that former U.S. president Ronald Reagan liked Russian proverbs. When Reagan was to visit President Gorbachev in Russia, Russian comedians changed very slightly an old Russian proverb meaning "Strike while the iron is hot." They changed the pronunciation just enough for the words to mean, "Get into Russia while there is still a Gorbachev."

## Folk Dancing and Music

Russian folk dances are performed by groups of people, rather than couples, and are usually very exciting and action packed. The traditional *Kazachock* dances are among the most popular. *Kazachok* is Russian for "Cossack" and refers to Russian soldiers who were famous for their horse-riding skills.

This Russian "Gypsy" dance is an example of the exuberant and energetic dances for which Russian folk dancers are famous.

"Venzelya" demonstrates the more common type of folk dance, one that involves groups of people. The dancers are Russian Americans from a Russian dance club in New York City.

The Cossacks were fierce warriors who developed their own style of dancing to show off their strength. The dances are difficult to perform because the men dance, kick out their legs, and leap into the air, all from a squatting position. Of course, there are easier Russian dances, too, that everyone can take part in.

Traditional songs range from tender love songs like "Dark Eyes" and "Kalinka" to the enthusiastic songs about life in Russia such as "Moscow Nights" and the "Volga Boat Song." It is clear from the many songs about the beauty of their homeland that Russians around the world remember their country with great fondness.

Russian folk songs are most often accompanied on the violin, the accordion, and the balalaika, which is similar to a triangular guitar with a flat back. There are actually six sizes of balalaika, each varying in tone from the others, and Russians have orchestras made up entirely of balalaikas.

The folk music matches the songs and dances. Most often, the music is full of life and action; sometimes it is tragic; sometimes it is romantic. Whatever the type of music, it is easy to feel the Russian folk artists' excitement and love for their homeland.

Although few Russian Americans perform the dances or sing many of the songs together these days, many of them eagerly go to performances by visiting Russian troupes or by folk dance clubs in America. When Americans attend these performances, they are seeing only a part of the Russian culture and its influence on our own in the United States.

Natalie Wood enthralled millions of Americans with her acting in many Hollywood movies from the 1940s until her death by drowning in 1981.

# CHAPTER SIX

# CONTRIBUTIONS TO AMERICAN CULTURE
## SO MUCH BY SO FEW

**R**ussians in the United States have given us lox and bagels, sour cream, lemon in our tea, beef stroganoff, vodka, borscht, and pumpernickel bread. To many Americans, these flavorful reminders of Russian culture may seem small compared with something else we have all around us, an invention that one Russian made possible — television.

## Russian Contributions to Technology

Vladimir Zworykin came to the United States from Russia after World War I. In the early 1930s, he invented the tube that made possible the first television, which was introduced in 1938. The world has not been the same since. We keep in touch with events happening around the planet — and even in space — while sitting in the comfort of our living rooms. Thanks to television and such advances in video technology as cable television, satellite transmission, video cassette recorders, and video games, we are entertained by everything from movies to sporting events, concerts, and a wide variety of commercial television programming, all at

Inventor Vladimir Zworykin works in his laboratory in 1926, looking for the technology that eventually gave us television.

relatively low cost. We can even shop or take college courses using the television.

In 1940, Vladimir Zworykin also invented the first electron microscope, which magnifies objects up to one hundred thousand times. Overnight, the fascinating world of cells became more visible to scientists and doctors, leading to further advances in medicine. Ordinary items such as household dust suddenly came to life, revealing life forms that no one had suspected existed and increasing our understanding of the world in which we live.

Similar advances were made by several Russian Americans in the medical field, including Theodosius Dobzhansky. He studied the genes inside fruit fly cells to increase our understanding of how characteristics are passed from one generation to another. Helena Fedukovicz, an eye surgeon,

helped increase our understanding and control of eye infections. And Solman Waksman discovered the bacterium that caused tuberculosis, a disease that used to be the leading cause of death in the United States until he also discovered a way to cure it.

## Science and Industry

Other Russian Americans have contributed greatly to developing sciences and industry in the United States. Some of us use electricity generated by nuclear power plants. These exist in part because George Gamow, a Russian who came to the United States in 1934, had ideas about atoms and their control that led to the idea of nuclear fission and thus nuclear energy. He was also an astronomer and applied his understanding of nuclear fission to help explain the evolution of stars.

On May 20, 1940, Igor Sikorsky, with his hat still firmly on his head, took his prototype helicopter for its first flight. The machine rose straight up thirty feet, flew two hundred feet around the airfield, and then landed safely.

When TV news crews relay live shots from inaccessible areas, medical teams airlift critically injured people to the hospital in minutes, or the military lands equipment and supplies in the middle of a jungle, we see nothing unusual in the transportation used. Leonardo da Vinci, the Italian Renaissance genius, may have dreamed of and even drawn a helicopter, but it took a Russian American, Igor Sikorsky, to make that dream a reality when he invented the VS 300 helicopter in 1939. The U.S. military still uses a helicopter named after Sikorsky.

A Russian who fled the revolution in 1917, Sikorsky was active in aircraft manufacturing soon after he arrived in the United States. By 1923, he had formed an aircraft manufacturing corporation that built one of the first twin-engine passenger planes to fly in the United States; it was able to carry fourteen passengers. A few years later, his company was building flying boats that could land on water, and by 1931, it had built the first large four-engine plane in the United States. A few years later, his company's planes were large and powerful enough to fly passengers across the Atlantic and Pacific oceans, revolutionizing international travel for a world divided by giant bodies of water, which previously could only be crossed by slow-moving steamships.

In a different field, Russian composer Vladimir Usazhevsky used his musical and scientific skills in 1947 to help conceive and design the equipment used to make electronic music. The new types of sound and their amplification opened the door to the pop groups that several generations of Americans have enjoyed during the last half of the twentieth century.

## Ballet

In addition to many inventions and scientific discoveries, Russians have brought much to the arts in the United States. When ballet is mentioned, many people think of Russian ballerinas and ballet dancers. The reason is simple: Russian Americans have been at the center of ballet in the United States since Michael Fokin introduced the free ballet style in 1925.

George Balanchine (center) demonstrates the correct "pas de deux" dance position for ballet dancers in 1950.

Mikhail Baryshnikov rehearses at the Kennedy Center with the American Ballet Theater in 1986. The Latvian-born dancer and choreographer who came to the U.S. from the Soviet Union is a master of classic Russian ballet.

in 1948 set up the New York City Ballet, creating over two hundred ballets for North America's best-known ballet theater.

The list of famous Russian ballerinas and ballet dancers in the U.S. is long and includes Natalia Makarova, Valery Banov, and Alexandra Danilova, all of whom may be familiar to older generations. Rudolf Nureyev, who died recently, is known to many younger Americans.

Thousands of Russian ballet dancers have immigrated to North America in just the last few years. Ballet companies throughout the United States, short of coaches and male dancers, have welcomed them with open arms. One of the most influential of the coaches is Irina Kolpakova, who used to be a prima ballerina with the Kirov ballet. These recent Russian arrivals bring to U.S. ballet the discipline and grace of the classic Vaganova style in which they have been trained. While they teach American dancers the Vaganova style, the Americans teach the Russians the faster and jazzier styles of modern ballet that they learned over the years from George Balanchine!

George Balanchine established the School of American Ballet in 1934, where he taught generations of Americans how to dance ballet and also matched dance movements to music, or choreographed, for both Hollywood and Broadway productions. He created the American Ballet Company and

Russians contribute to theater and dance not only as performers, but backstage as well. Russian Boris Aronson, for example, designed the stage settings for more than a hundred plays, ballets, and operas performed in the United States.

## Music

The modern classical music scene has been heavily influenced by Russians who settled in the United States. Igor Stravinsky was an inspiration to American composers such as Aaron Copland, and his ballets are masterpieces that have profoundly influenced American music.

Another great composer who provided generations of Americans with pleasurable music was Sergei Rachmaninoff. He arrived in the United States after the Russian Revolution and composed operas, symphonies, piano concertos, and numerous other works from his home in Beverly Hills.

Russian conductors have helped make U.S. orchestras among the best in the world. Serge Koussevitsky, who worked with the Boston Symphony Orchestra, Mstislav Rostropovich, who directed the National Symphony Orchestra in Washington, D.C., and Nicholas Sokomoff, with the Cleveland Orchestra, are most famous among Russian conductors who have contributed their talents to shaping American culture.

Mstislav Rostropovich is also a virtuoso cellist, one among many Russian American master performers. Isaac Stern and Yehudi Menuhin are household names to lovers of classical music in America. They were born to Russian Jewish parents in Russia and New York City, respectively, and are admired for

Composer Igor Stravinsky conducts a rehearsal in New York City's Center Theater in 1947.

A young Isaac Stern concentrates during a virtuoso performance on his violin.

**Composer Irving Berlin wrote hundreds of songs that have become mainstays of American popular music.**

Irving Berlin, another Jewish Russian American, wrote hundreds of popular songs that became classics in the United States. "White Christmas," "Easter Parade," and "Annie Get Your Gun" are some of Berlin's best-known scores. His "God Bless America" is a familiar anthem at political rallies as well as concerts.

"American Rhapsody" was written by violinist and composer Efram Zimbalist. Another Russian American, Louis Gruenberg, was the first composer to combine jazz and symphony music. Dimitri Tionkin settled in Los Angeles in 1925 and wrote many scores for Hollywood movies. "The Old Man and The Sea," "The High and the Mighty," "High Noon," and "The Great Waltz" are some of his better-known works.

their superb violin performances. The pianist Vladimir Horowitz and violinist Mischa Elman are in the same category. All four have made many recordings of classical music and set examples for American musicians today of the high standards they, too, can reach.

## Drama

Some of America's greatest actors, including Marlon Brando, Paul Newman, and Al Pacino, were trained at The Actors' Studio in New York. The acting method used there was strongly influenced by Rus-

## THE RUSSIAN LANGUAGE IN THE UNITED STATES

Some Russian words or phrases have been absorbed into American English, including *perestroika* (economic and political reforms), *glasnost* (greater social and political freedom), *pogrom* (massacre or persecution), *gulag* (forced-labor camp), *vodka, stroganoff,* and *czar* (leader or director; for example, a "drug czar" is appointed to direct an anti-drug-abuse campaign).

The word *babushka* is sometimes heard in the United States as a term for a grandmother. It originally refers to the scarf that grandmothers used to wear — and often still do wear — on their head.

Occasionally, when an American wants to sound Russian, he or she may jokingly add the Russian syllable "ski" to the end of a word, which usually adds no meaning to the word itself. Russians, on the other hand, take many English words and use them in their own language.

sian American director Konstantin Stanislavsky. He had actors practice the emotions of the character they were portraying and improvise things that person would do or say.

Natalie Wood was a well-loved movie and television star of Russian descent who from the age of six acted in over forty movies, such as *Miracle on 34th Street, Rebel Without a Cause, West Side Story,* and *Gypsy,* in which she acted the part of the young Gypsy Rose Lee.

### Literature

Russia has a rich literary history, and many Russian Americans have continued this tradition as novelists. The most prolific was Isaac Asimov, an Odessa-born Jew whose science fiction works, such as *The Foundation Trilogy*, as well as his many works on science, helped make difficult scientific ideas understandable and exciting for young and old alike. In all, Asimov wrote five hundred books on subjects as diverse as history, science, and the Bible, in addition to mystery stories.

**World-renowned Russian author Aleksandr Solzhenitsyn lived in the States for many years in exile. He returned to Russia following the collapse of the Soviet Union in the 1990s.**

Poet Joseph Brodsky in 1987, just after he heard the news that he had won the Nobel Prize in literature.

thought and viewed their lives. Among the best known are Ayn Rand *(Atlas Shrugged)*, Saul Bellow *(Humbolt's Gift)*, and Vladimir Nabokov *(Lolita)*. Saul Bellow earned the Pulitzer Prize for fiction and the Nobel Prize in literature in 1976. The poet Joseph Brodsky was also awarded the Nobel Prize in literature in 1987 and named the Poet Laureate of the United States in 1991.

## Promoting Peace through Culture

Sol Hurok was an American of Russian Jewish descent who did much to ease tensions between the United States and the Soviet Union during the Cold War through cultural exchanges. He sponsored tours in the United States for many famous artists like the Russian ballerina Anna Pavlova and companies like the Russian Ballet Theater. He also arranged for American performers to tour the Soviet Union, all in the belief that the more communication there was between the two countries, the less likely they were to declare war against each other. In fact, during the Cuban missile crisis in 1962, when the United States and Soviet Union were on the verge of war over the presence of Soviet missiles in Cuba, a Russian ballet company continued to tour the United States under Hurok's name.

Aleksandr Solzhenitsyn is another well-known Russian author who lived in the United States until very recently in self-imposed isolation. He wrote many novels, such as *First Circle, Cancer Ward,* and *The Gulag Archipelago,* that criticized the oppressive communist system in the Soviet Union. His writing and campaigning helped educate Americans on the prison camps and human rights abuses of Soviet communism.

There were other authors who wrote books that influenced the way Americans

## A Small Group That Has Given Much

When Russians arrived in the United States, they came from different backgrounds and for different reasons. As a result, they have not formed a single, recognizable group. They have not created nationally recognized celebrations such as Oktoberfest or St. Patrick's Day as the Germans and Irish have done. These factors make it difficult for Russian Americans to project their culture to other Americans, as well as making it harder to bring Russian Americans together as a group.

Despite this lack of organization and focus, many Americans of Russian descent are strongly attracted to their culture and seek to experience it whenever the occasion arises. There is a longing for the Russia of old: the beautiful countryside, the music, the literature, and the folk traditions. This urge keeps Russian culture alive in the United States. Russian churches continue to preserve Russian culture as well by bringing Russian Americans to their services and providing Sunday schools that interest the children.

The United States used to be called a melting pot, in which the people from different lands let go of their cultures to become Americans. Today, America is considered more like a giant salad bowl, in

The dynamic Anna Pavlova, seen here in 1909, helped popularize Russian ballet in the West during the years following the Russian Revolution.

which the different cultures provide a variety of tastes and colors to make the salad more interesting. As Russian immigrants go through the inevitable process of becoming Americans, they bring with them ideas and skills that make our culture that much more exciting and pleasurable for all.

# CHRONOLOGY

**1741**    The first Russians land on Alaskan soil, on Kayak Island.

**1748**    The first Russian settlement in North America is established in Three Saints Bay, Alaska, with 191 men and a woman.

**1785**    Grigory Shelikhov establishes the first Russian school at Three Saints Bay and instructs Native Alaskans in Russian, arithmetic, and Christianity.

**1790**    The first marriage between a Russian and a Native woman takes place on Kodiak Island.

**1792**    The first Russian Orthodox church in North America, St. Nicholas, is built near present-day Anchorage, Alaska.

**1806**    Russian Nicholas Razanov sails to San Francisco.

**1812**    Fort Ross is established, the first Russian settlement in California.

**1840**    Bishop Veniaminov, the first Russian Orthodox bishop in North America, is appointed.

**1841**    The Russians sell Fort Ross and leave California.

**1844**    The Russian Orthodox Cathedral of St. Michael is built in Sitka, Alaska.

**1867**    The United States buys Alaska from Russia for 7.2 million dollars; although this amounted to only about two cents an acre, the sale was ridiculed in the United States and referred to as "Seward's Folly" in mocking tribute to William Seward, the U.S. secretary of state who negotiated the deal with Russia.

**1881**    The Russian Orthodox Cathedral is completed in San Francisco.

**1888**    Peter Dementiev establishes the town of St. Petersburg in Florida after building a railroad there.

**1898**    A Russian Orthodox Missionary School is opened in Minneapolis, Minnesota.

**1900**    Increased unrest in Russia increases emigration to the United States for the next two decades.

**1905**    The Russian Orthodox Church's headquarters is moved from San Francisco to New York City.

**1907**    The Russian Orthodox Catholic Women's Mutual Aid Society is founded in Pittsburgh, Pennsylvania.

**1910**    *New Russian Word,* the oldest Russian American newspaper in existence, is founded in New York City.

**1917**    The Russian Revolution begins; the resulting upheaval of Russian society will result in the forming of the Soviet Union in 1922, a nation made up of Russia and many other republics that were formerly independent nations.

**1918**    The first refugees from the Russian Revolution arrive in the United States.

**1920**    Russian Orthodox priests in the United States cut all ties with the Russian Orthodox Church in Moscow.

**1925**    Michael Fokine brings Russian Ballet to North America.

**1938**    Vladimir Zworykin develops the electronic system leading to the invention of television.

**1939**    The Tolstoy Foundation is established in New York for the purpose of assisting refugees from the Soviet Union.

**1939**    Igor Sikorsky invents the first successful helicopter built in the West.

**1940**    Vladimir Zworykin invents the first electron microscope, which magnifies up to one hundred thousand times.

**1947**    Vladimir Usazhevsky, a Russian American composer, helps develop modern electronic music.

| 1948 | George Balanchine establishes the New York City Ballet. |
|---|---|
| 1949 | Russians living in China flee the new communist government and settle in San Francisco. |
| 1951 | The last of the Soviet refugees from World War II emigrate to the United States. |
| 1960s-1970s | Large numbers of Soviet Jews, many allowed to leave on the pretext of going to Israel, emigrate to the United States; many Soviet dissidents also manage to leave for the United States. |
| 1973 | The Congress of Russian Americans is formed. |
| 1985 | Mikhail Gorbachov becomes general secretary — and eventually president — of the Soviet Union. |
| 1991 | Joseph Brodsky named U.S. Poet Laureate; the Soviet Union dissolves as a unified nation of socialist republics; Russia and the other republics making up the former U.S.S.R. are now independent nations; emigration of Russians to United States increases. |

# GLOSSARY

**Balalaika** A Russian stringed instrument similar to a guitar, with a triangular shape and a flat back.

**Chaperone** In traditional Greek culture, the practice of an older or married woman escorting a younger woman or girl when she goes out to parties and other social occasions.

**Communism** A system of government and social organization in which all property and goods are owned by the government and shared equally by all the people in the society. The government of the former Soviet Union was based on this system.

**Conscientious objector** A person who refuses to joined the armed forces because he or she thinks it is wrong to kill others. Conscientious objectors object to war on the basis of their conscience, or their feeling about the difference between right and wrong.

**Conscription** The draft; mandatory enrollment into the armed forces, often in time of war.

**Culture** The ideas, customs, and art that a group of people share.

**Dowry** Money and possessions brought by a woman to the man she marries. Dowries are no longer in general use in the United States.

**Eastern Orthodox Church** A branch of Christianity that includes the Russian Orthodox Church and the Greek Orthodox Church and observes strictly the original writings and teachings of the early Church. *Orthodox* means adhering to a traditional or accepted faith, especially religion.

**Foundry** A place where metal or glass is melted and formed into shapes.

**Interest** A small amount of money that a borrower pays to a lender for the privilege of using the lender's money.

**Lent** A period in the Christian calendar prior to Easter when Christians fast for forty weekdays to commemorate Jesus' fasting.

**Making ends meet** Attempting to survive financially on whatever money is available.

**Mennonite** Christian denomination founded in 1525 and named for Dutch religious leader Menno Simons. Some Mennonites lived in Russia before emigrating to the United States.

| | |
|---|---|
| **Minority** | A group of people — known as a minority because they are fewer in number than those who make up the mainstream society or culture — who share some characteristic, such as race, religion, or ethnicity, that sets them apart from most of the people around them in that society. |
| **Molokans** | A group of Russian Protestants who broke away from the Russian Orthodox Church in the eighteenth century. |
| **Nobility** | The people in a country who hold titles and high rank, such as royalty. |
| **Politics** | The art and profession of holding public office and of gaining and using power in countries and groups. |
| **Ruble** | A unit of money used in Russia. |
| **Russians** | The descendants of the ancient Slavs who moved out of Eastern Europe into present-day Russia two thousand years ago |
| **Russian Orthodox Church** | One of several national branches of the Eastern Orthodox Church. |
| **Serf** | A peasant who worked for and was considered the property of a landowner. |
| **Slavic** | Eastern European peoples and the languages they speak, including Russians, Czechs, Slovaks, Poles, Serbs, and Croatians. |
| **Soviet** | A governing council elected at the local, regional, or national level. |
| **Soviet Union** | The Union of Soviet Socialist Republics, or U.S.S.R., which was formed in 1922 with the union of Russia and several other formerly independent republics, such as Belarus and the Ukraine. The Soviet Union was ruled by the communist government that took power in Russia following the Russian Revolution in 1917. The Soviet Union was dissolved in 1991. |
| **Spiritual** | Concerning the inner life or soul of human beings. |
| **Tenement** | A large apartment building, often crowded, rundown, and occupied by people with little money. |
| **Tundra** | A large, flat area of land with no trees where the ground is always frozen below the topsoil. |

# FURTHER READING

Buettner, Don. *A Journey by Bicycle Across Southern Russia.* Minneapolis: Lerner Publications, 1994.

Eubank, Nancy. *The Russians in America.* Minneapolis: Lerner Publications, 1973.

Gerber, Stanford. *Reusskoya Celo.* New York: AMS Press, 1985.

Gillies, John. *The New Russia.* New York: Macmillan Child Group, 1994.

Magosci, Paul R. *The Russian Americans.* New York: Chelsea House, 1989.

Perrin, Penelope. *Russia.* New York: Macmillan Child Group, 1994.

Werdsman, Vladimir. *The Russians in America.* Dobbs Ferry: Oceana Publications, 1979.

# INDEX